T0385448

SIMPSON

IMPRINT IN HUMANITIES

The humanities endowment
by Sharon Hanley Simpson and
Barclay Simpson honors
MURIEL CARTER HANLEY
whose intellect and sensitivity
have enriched the many lives
that she has touched.

The publisher and the University of California Press Foundation gratefully acknowledge the generous support of the Simpson Imprint in Humanities.

The Clarion of Syria

The Clarion of Syria

A Patriot's Call against the Civil War of 1860

Butrus al-Bustani

Introduced and Translated by
Jens Hanssen and Hicham Safieddine
Foreword by Ussama Makdisi

UNIVERSITY OF CALIFORNIA PRESS

University of California Press, one of the most distinguished university presses in the United States, enriches lives around the world by advancing scholarship in the humanities, social sciences, and natural sciences. Its activities are supported by the UC Press Foundation and by philanthropic contributions from individuals and institutions. For more information, visit www.ucpress.edu.

University of California Press
Oakland, California

Library of Congress Cataloging-in-Publication Data

Names: Hanssen, Jens, author & translator. | Safieddine, Hicham, author & translator. | Makdisi, Ussama Samir, 1968- writer of foreword. | Container of (expression): Bustani, Butrus ibn Bulus, 1818 or 1819–1882 or 1883. Nafir Suriyah. English.

Title: The Clarion of Syria : a patriot's call against the civil war of 1860 / by Butrus Al-Bustani ; translated by Jens Hanssen and Hicham Safieddine; foreword by Ussama Makdisi.

Description: Oakland, California : University of California Press, 2019 | Includes bibliographical references and index. | This work is licensed under a Creative Commons CC-BY-NC-ND license. To view a copy of the license, visit: http://creativecommons.org/licenses |

Identifiers: LCCN 2018048201 (print) | LCCN 2018052309 (ebook) | ISBN 9780520971158 (Epub) | ISBN 9780520299436 (pbk. : alk. paper)

Subjects: LCSH: Bustani, Butrus ibn Bulus, 1818 or 1819–1882 or 1883. Nafir Suriyah. | Bustani, Butrus ibn Bulus, 1818 or 1819–1882 or 1883. | Syria—History—19th century.

Classification: LCC PN5449.L42 (ebook) | LCC PN5449.L42 B87 2019 (print) | DDC 079.5691—dc23

LC record available at https://lccn.loc.gov/2018048201

28 27 26 25 24 23 22 21 20 19
10 9 8 7 6 5 4 3 2 1

The worst thing under the firmament is war, and the most horrendous among them are civil wars.

Nafir Suriyya, Clarion 5, November 1, 1860

CONTENTS

Acknowledgments xi

Foreword by Ussama Makdisi xiii

Introduction: Translating Civil War
Jens Hanssen and Hicham Safieddine

1

PART I: THE CLARION OF SYRIA: THE CONTEXT

Chapter 1: The War of 1860: Roots and Ramifications
Jens Hanssen and Hicham Safieddine

13

Chapter 2: Butrus al-Bustani: From Protestant Convert
to Ottoman Patriot and Arab Reformer
Jens Hanssen and Hicham Safieddine

23

Chapter 3: *Nafir Suriyya* in Arab Historiography
Jens Hanssen

35

Chapter 4: Toward a Conceptual History
of *Nafir Suriyya*
Jens Hanssen
45

Chapter 5: *Wataniyya* as Antidote to Sectarianism
Jens Hanssen
53

PART II: TRANSLATION OF THE CLARION OF SYRIA

Chapter 6: Clarion 1
65

Chapter 7: Clarion 2
68

Chapter 8: Clarion 3
71

Chapter 9: Clarion 4
76

Chapter 10: Clarion 5
80

Chapter 11: Clarion 6
85

Chapter 12: Clarion 7
92

Chapter 13: Clarion 8
98

Chapter 14: Clarion 9
105

Chapter 15: Clarion 10
114

Chapter 16: Clarion 11
122

Notes 131

References 149

Index 163

ACKNOWLEDGMENTS

Translations of historical texts like *The Clarion of Syria* are labors of love, and perhaps literary betrayals, that bequeath valuable lessons for our present. In bringing Butrus al-Bustani's bygone reflection on civil war to light, our first thanks go to Niels Hooper, executive editor at the University of California Press, for having recognized early on the contemporary significance of this project, and for having seen it go through many iterations to the end. We are also grateful for the insightful comments we received from the blind reviewers of the manuscript. May this publication lead to more translations of modern Arabic social and literary thought.

We are particularly excited about the fact that in addition to a hard copy, this work will be published as an e-book with open access. This will make a canonical text of Arab cultural heritage accessible for the first time—and for free—to an English audience in classrooms and broader communities and publics. The e-project was made possible thanks to generous funding by Rice University's Humanities Research Center (HRC), headed by Farès el-Dahdah, and generous donations by Arwa and Aziz Shaibani, as well as Dania Dandashly. We greatly value their unwavering commitment to supporting Arab studies. We also appreciate the support of Ussama Makdisi, who, in his capacity as Arab-American Educational Foundation Professor in Arabic Studies at Rice University, endorsed our application for funding from HRC and agreed to write a foreword. Special thanks go to the staff at the University of California Press, particularly Robert Demke, Bradley Depew, Sabrina Robleh, and Emilia Thiuri, who have worked hard on editing our manuscript into shape and seeing it seamlessly through the production process. Our indexer, Linda Christian, has been a pleasure to work with, too.

Our translated text and the accompanying contextualization offer one interpretation. We have tried to stay as loyal to the original meaning as possible. We take responsibility for any infelicities that the reader may detect and hope that our book encourages further critical debates on how best to represent the experience of past Arab intellectuals for future generations.

FOREWORD

The Protestant educator journalist and encyclopedist Butrus al-Bustani was one of the great luminaries of the Arabic renaissance of the nineteenth century. His seminal pamphlets collectively known as *Nafir Suriyya* were published in the immediate aftermath of the sectarian crisis of 1860 in Mount Lebanon and Damascus. They exhorted the inhabitants of Syria to unite, to eschew sectarian fanaticism, and to think critically about self and other. Jens Hanssen and Hicham Safieddine's translation of *Nafir Suriyya* is excellent. It provides English-language readers a long overdue window into the very beginnings of what we might call an unrecognized antisectarian tradition in the Arab world. To talk about antisectarianism is, of course, to suggest a new way of thinking about an often Orientalized region. Rather than seeing it as a place of eternal sectarian conflict, it seems so much more interesting to see the Arab world as a place, beginning in 1860, of constant willed work on the part of men and women who have grappled with the problem of politicized religious or ethnic difference.

For well over a century, Arabs (and their non-Arab counterparts across the region) have fought against the scourge of sectarianism in a manner analogous to how South Asians have fought against communalism, and how Americans have fought against racism. Both sectarianism and antisectarianism are habits of the mind as much as they are political, social, or economic practices.

The exhortations in *Nafir Suriyya* to national unity anticipate the great question of secular affiliation that every Arab subject of the modern era has had to face: how to reconcile the principle of secular equality with the historic reality of religious and ethnic diversity; how to do so at a time of constant Western imperialism and interventionism that relentlessly exploit this diversity; and how to do so in the face of the terrible expressions of sectarian fanaticism that constantly undermine the ability of Arabs to create a society greater than the sum of their communal parts. The ecumenical Bustani understood what many in the contemporary Arab world still understand: that each of us, as individuals, has a choice to make about how to affiliate with our diverse world. We can read the world in sectarian terms or in secular ones. We can choose to be part of an emancipatory project or a repressive one. Both choices can be rationalized, but only one can ultimately lead to a more just and egalitarian world.

Ussama Makdisi

Houston, September 2018

Introduction

Translating Civil War

JENS HANSSEN AND HICHAM SAFIEDDINE

> News of the spell of atrocities and abominations committed this
> summer by the troublemakers in our midst has reached the corners
> of the Earth. All over the civilized world, it has drawn pity and
> gloom on one hand, and anger and wrath on the other.

With these opening lines, *Nafīr Suriyya—The Clarion of Syria—*
launched its urgent appeal to overcome the civil war in Mount
Lebanon and Damascus in the summer of 1860, and to rebuild
Syrian society in the war's aftermath. This key text of the
Nahda—the nineteenth-century Arabic reform and revival
movement—has recently received renewed popular and scholarly attention.[1] At the time of its publication, *Nafīr Suriyya* ran
as a series of eleven pamphlets by an anonymous author from
September 1860 to April 1861.[2] The pamphlets did not present a
detailed litany of atrocities, which other contemporary eyewitnesses provided.[3] Rather, they addressed an array of universally

resonant and locally relevant themes that render the pamphlets pertinent beyond their immediate context. With a style oscillating between Paulinian sermon and Socratic dialogue, the author ponders the meaning of civil war in relation to religion, politics, morality, society, and civilization.

The author expresses gratitude for European intervention but warns in passing of its potential long-term harm. Key passages evince a subtle understanding of the rights of "man" on the one hand, and a bourgeois deference to the rule of law and political authority on the other. The pamphlets also advocate the twin prerogatives of opposing separation between people of the same homeland based on religion or kinship and proposing the separation of religious and political authority; they espouse an Ottoman reformism that affirms loyalty to the imperial center but calls for the rulers to attend to the welfare of their subjects. Other passages grapple with the task of refuting Orientalist stereotypes about Arabs while at the same time embracing some of its underlying assumptions. Still others extol the value of Western civilization and its racialized hierarchy of nations but warn against superficial emulation. Above all, *Nafīr Sūriyya* was an antisectarian clarion call to build a cohesive and "civilized" Syrian society in place of what the author considered a community riven with the most pernicious of conflicts, violent fanaticism, and factionalism. As the author put it:

> The worst thing under the firmament is war, and the most horrendous among them are civil wars, which break out between people of a single country and which are often triggered by trivial causes and for ignoble aims. (*Nafīr Sūriyya 5*, November 1, 1860)

Current impressions of Yemen, Libya, and Syria to the contrary, civil wars are not a particularly more common occurrence in

Middle Eastern history compared to other regions.[4] But as is the case in other parts of the world, past conflicts that would qualify as civil wars by today's standards cast very long shadows into the present. One example is the Battle of the Camel, which broke out in 656 AD and marked one of the first wars between Muslim armies. Even though it was a war over worldly succession that took place over a millennium ago, it continues to be invoked to incite sectarian strife and explain contemporary Sunni-Shia rivalries.[5] The memory of foreign invasions, too, continues to haunt the Arab world. The sackings of Jerusalem by Crusaders in 1099 and of Baghdad by Mongols in 1258 had their apocalyptic chroniclers whose lamentations have resurfaced repeatedly since American-led armies started the current destruction of Iraq in 2003.[6] In the modern period, revolutions were often derided as civil wars by conservatives or royalists.[7] Some conflicts that came to be labeled "civil wars" were, in fact, state pogroms (like the Young Turk genocide of Anatolian Armenians during World War I), settler-colonial conquests (like the Zionist ethnic cleansing of Palestine in 1948), or wars of independence, most notably the Algerian liberation struggle against colonial France (1954–62).[8]

The French invasion of Egypt in 1798 gave modern Arab intellectual history its colonial frame.[9] At the time, however, Napoleon's army elicited an entertaining mixture of opprobrium and ridicule. The chroniclers 'Abd al-Rahman al-Jabarti and Hasan al-'Attar believed Napoleon's rhetoric of liberating Egyptians from Mamluk oppression no more than the Iraqis greeted US soldiers with flowers in 2003.[10] By contrast, the *Nakba* of Palestine in 1948 prompted Constantin Zurayk's famous call in his *The Meaning of Disaster* for a fundamental social, political, and military transformation of the Arab world in order to survive and compete against the persistence of imperialism and the success of Zionism.[11] The subsequent Arab military defeat in 1967 generated Sadik al-ʿAzm's *Self-Criticism after the Defeat,* in which he blamed the lack of a sustained intellectual response on, among other things, the Arabs' purported "clever personality" syndrome, or *al-fahlawiyyah.* Despite the ideological differences between Zurayq and al-ʿAzm, as well as the latter's orientalist psychologizing, both authors warned that Arab defeats were partly a symptom of deeper social ills. They implored their readers to take the catastrophes as wake-up calls to expose the bankruptcy of existing regimes and build progressive societies capable of autonomous and equitable national development.[12]

Its specific historical context notwithstanding, the eleven pamphlets that made up *Nafir Suriyya* anticipated the ambivalence of introspection found in Zurayq's and al-ʿAzm's texts. Its anonymous author had to deal with civil war—"the most disparaged of all wars"[13]—and the specter of European encroachment. What elicited particular concern on the pages of *Nafir Suriyya* were the ominous signs that before "fellow countrymen" could become good neighbors again, the purportedly empathetic European eyewitness would turn into military saviors and suspend the process of social healing indefinitely. While *Nafir Suriyya* grappled with the civil war in Mount Lebanon and the ensuing Bab Tuma massacre in Damascus, the full diplomatic and journalistic force of Great Power rivalry on the Eastern Mediterranean shores unleashed the first international humanitarian intervention of its kind.[14]

The duplicity and opportunism of this intervention by European imperial powers during the "Syrian disturbances" are largely absent from al-Bustani's account. But they were astutely dissected at the time by Karl Marx in one of his regular dispatches to the *New York Daily Tribune*.[15] The author of *Nafīr Suriyya* appreciated and generally ascribed noble motives to Ottoman, European, and American intervention. By contrast, Marx noted that the French press feigned outrage at the disturbances and supported Napoleon III's designs of pacification by annexation, and that the Russian government, too, favored military intervention to deflect from domestic troubles. Four years after the Crimean War, it was evident according to Marx "that the autocrat of France and the autocrat of Russia, laboring under the same urgent necessity of sounding the war-trumpet, act in common concert." Meanwhile, the Prussian government was opposed to military action but, Marx opined, only because a Prussian adventure in Syria would put in jeopardy the project of German unification.[16] Despite his scathing critique of foreign power intervention and connivance, Marx shared the biases of the liberal press and the conservative politicians about the "barbarous clans of the Lebanon" as he ended his article with a damning judgment of international incitement and local political pathologies:

> In respect to England I will only add, that, in 1841, Lord Palmerston furnished the Druses with the arms they kept ever since, and that, in 1846, by a convention with the Czar Nicholas, he abolished, in point of fact, the Turkish sway that curbed the wild tribes of the Lebanon, and stipulated for them a quasi-independence which, in the run of time, and under the proper management of foreign plotters, could only beget a harvest of blood.[17]

In light of even the most astute European commentators' reductionist assumptions about the local "wild tribes" of 1860s, the historical and literary significance of *Nafīr Suriyya* cannot be overestimated. *Nafīr Suriyya*'s author evokes the language of "tribalism," but as part of a more elaborate critique of the local dimensions of the civil war that befell his homeland. Civil wars rarely speak their names. Frequently, euphemisms like "disturbances," "troubles," or just "events" mask the atrocities committed and the modern forces that produced them. Lebanon and Syria are no exception. *Nafir Suriyya* used *al-khirba* (ruinous event) and the more conventional label *al-fitna*, which is invoked today to refer to the "discord" of 656–80 that supposedly begot perennial Sunnis-Shia rivalry.[18] More significantly, *Nafir Suriyya* also introduced the term *civil war (al-harb al-ahliyya)*.[19] This neologism gestured toward two important aspects that set 1860 apart from previous conceptions of communal violence: it was "civil" in that the violence was carried out between fellow inhabitants, by armed civilians on unarmed civilians; and it was a "war" because of its scale and international dimension. For *Nafir Suriyya*'s author, this was a social conflict carried out by military means at a time when communal feuds and factionalism were supposed to have been superseded by the march of history and by people's recognition of the human interdependence in modern society. The civil war has led—he laments—to human suffering and material loss, to mass dispersion of people, forced and voluntary exile, and widespread "homesickness" among fugitive victims and perpetrators alike. Even as the immediacy of the civil war and its author's evolving subjectivity make *The Clarion of Syria* a visceral, contradictory, at times repetitive, and always challenging text to read, it evinces a profound and painful hermeneutic process on the part of its author that was unprecedented in Arabic literature and remarkable by any standard for its time.

It is unclear when exactly the identity of the pamphlets' author—a "patriot"—was revealed. Contemporary obituaries of one of the leading intellectuals and scholars in Beirut, Butrus al-Bustani, indicate he was known to be behind these pamphlets during his lifetime. He himself claimed authorship of *Nafir Suriyya* in the entry for *nafara* in *Muhit al-Muhit* (1867). Born into a socially reputable Maronite family in 1819, al-Bustani came into contact with American missionaries around 1840, which shaped his thinking throughout his life. In the 1850s, he worked as a dragoman for the American consul. It is no surprise then that al-Bustani's *Nafir Suriyya* shared a civilizational discourse with foundational Euro-American texts that cut across geography, culture, genre, and style. Its ardent patriotic tone, if not content, resonates in part with "The Address to the German Nation," which Johann Gottlieb Fichte penned in Berlin during the French occupation in 1807, and in some respects with Simón Bolívar's "Jamaican Letter" of 1815, which later became a South American independence manifesto. Perhaps a more accurate analogy with Romantic idealism is Heinrich Heine whose love-hate relationship with fellow Germans and Jews resonates with *Nafir Suriyya*'s concern for— and scathing critique of—Syrians' purported lack of self-respect, misplaced sense of honor, and violent intolerance. *Nafir Suriyya*'s invocation of the promise of civilization and the threat of barbarism also conjures up the conservative elitism of Matthew Arnold's *Culture and Anarchy* (1867) and of Domingo Sarmiento's liberal autobiographical novel and political manifesto for a strong Argentinian state, *Facundo* (1845).[20]

After the civil war in 1860, al-Bustani dedicated his life to Arab history, literature, and language. He founded schools, newspapers, encyclopaedias, and dictionaries. When he died in May 1883, his obituaries listed *Nafir Suriyya* among his major literary achievements.[21] One year later, his son Salim also passed away. The death of the Bustanis marked a downturn in Beirut's *Nahda*. Starting in the late 1870s, the Ottoman sultan Abdülhamid II's regime clamped down on political activism in Beirut. The press came to be censored, and many journalists left for British-occupied Egypt, where they embraced the new scientific outlooks: Darwinism, materialism, and socialism.[22] Finally in 1886, the Ottoman authorities closed the flagship of the al-Bustani family's intellectual enterprise, *al-Jinan,* apparently because of a glowing editorial by al-Bustani's son, Najib, in praise of the sultan's erstwhile nemesis Midhat Pasha, who had been the architect of the Ottoman constitution and governor general of Syria in the late 1870s.[23] American missionaries at the Syrian Protestant College, too, had clamped down on the liberal aspirations of students and some faculty. English became the language of instruction. This was anathema to al-Bustani, who had insisted in *Nafir Suriyya* on Arabic as the unifying language of education. Moreover, the college administration sacked a recently hired chemistry professor for challenging Christian creationism and endorsing Charles Darwin's and Charles Leil's ideas on evolutionary biology.[24]

These new political, economic, and cultural developments from the early 1880s onward challenged the way the Bustanis' and their contemporaries viewed their role as public intellectuals. New Imperialism and the attendant discourses of race threatened but did not eliminate the Bustanis' "ecumenical humanism"—to use Ussama Makdisi's evocative phrase.[25] These sociopolitical transformations had a profound effect on the Arabic language, not least because some experimental vocabulary disappeared while many terms changed their meaning. The role of al-Bustani in reviving and revising modern Arabic, partly through translation, is undeniable.[26] Translation was the activity that characterized all phases of his life. As a boy, he studied classical and modern languages extensively; later in life, he

helped translate the Bible into Arabic before serving as a dragoman for the US consulate; he edited al-Mutanabbi's *Diwan* and
translated Defoe's *Robinson Crusoe*. As the host of many literary
societies and founding editor of *al-Jinan* he dedicated himself to
the dissemination of historical knowledge and foreign ideas. As
a lexicographer, he defined the meanings of terms and pinned
down the semantic structure of Arabic; and as a cultural entre-
preneur he made available a concise history of the world in the
homes of educated Arabs.

His mastery of Arabic notwithstanding, al-Bustani struggled
to find the right language to translate the horrors of the civil
war into lessons learned. For us, the task of rendering his interpretation legible in English more than a century and a half later
was a double struggle of translating text and context. To address
this twin challenge, the book is divided into two parts. Part 1
provides context—historical, conceptual, and biographical—to
the war, the work at hand, and its author. Part 2, beginning with
chapter 6, offers the first full translation of all eleven pamphlets.
In part 1, the first chapter outlines the socioeconomic and political conditions that underlie the civil strife of 1860. Contrary to
what al-Bustani suggested in *Nafir Suriyya,* the war was much
more than a product of communal hatred and sectarian prejudice triggered by "trivial causes." Elite rivalries, class conflict,
imperial reform, and foreign intervention planted the seeds for
an all-out violent conflagration and stoked its fire afterward.
These complex social transformations left their deep mark on
al-Bustani's own life trajectory, which we chart in chapter 3. We
highlight al-Bustani's religious conversion, literary innovation,
and cultural contribution through his writings and educational
activity, all of which turned him into a key figure of the nineteenth-century *Nahda*. Chapter 4 discusses the historiography

that produced different scholarly articulations of the *Nahda* through diverse interpretations of *Nafir Suriyya* and its meaning. We close our contextual section with a conceptual study of the etymological origins and sociopolitical significance of al-Bustani's innovative terminology, such as *nafir, gharadh, al-harb al-ahliyya,* and most prominently, *al-watan.* This last term lay at the heart of a new lexicon of communal belonging and patriotism that al-Bustani and other Arab reformers of his time sought to instill in their interlocutors. Far from the chauvinistic nationalism that might be conjured up today, al-Bustani invoked love of the homeland—as we elaborate in chapter 5—as an antisectarian panacea, a necessary individual and collective disposition to build an inclusive postwar society, with all its utopian promises and concrete contradictions.

PART I

The Clarion of Syria

The Context

CHAPTER 1

The War of 1860

Roots and Ramifications

JENS HANSSEN AND HICHAM SAFIEDDINE

The idea of an independent Lebanon stretching back to early Ottoman times has more to do with the work of historians than with geographical or social givens of history. From the Maronite patriarch Istifan al-Duwayhi (1629–1704) to prominent scholar Kamal Salibi (1929–2011), historians of Lebanon have focused on the Druze-Maronite rivalry as one of the primordial driving forces behind the crystallization of modern Lebanon. Two formative periods according to this narrative were the reign of Fakhr al-Din II al-Maʿani (1572–1635) and the later Shihabi emirate (1789–1840). This approach wrote out of Lebanon's history ruling families of other denominations and the populations of the areas surrounding what became Mt. Lebanon in the late eighteenth century.[1] Only recently has the rule of Shiʿa vassals such as the Hamadas in the northern districts of Mt. Lebanon been studied critically.[2] It lasted, unevenly, for much of the seventeenth century and finally ended when the Ottoman army marched against the Hamadas in 1693–94 and forced them to retreat to the Bekaʿ Valley in the east and Bilad Bishara in the south. The Shihabi emirs stepped into this political void, encouraged Maronite settlement in Kisrawan, and built an effective tax-collecting statelet for the Druze and Maronite notability. Privileging the Druze-Maronite rivalry has also obscured the socioeconomic integration and political overlap between the coastal and mountainous regions and the rest of Syria, or Bilad al-Sham. The relative autonomy of Shihabi-ruled Mt. Lebanon was no exception in what Albert Hourani memorably labeled the golden age of the Ottoman politics of notables in the eighteenth century. The emirate coexisted alongside al-ʿAzm family-rule in Damascus and Zahir al-ʿUmar's and Ahmad Pasha al-Jazzar's reign in Acre.[3]

Nahda-era historians consecrated the *Sonderweg* narrative of an independent Shihabi emirate. For example, Nasif al-Yaziji's historical treatise on the feudal conditions of Mt. Lebanon completed in 1833, elided the wider Ottoman context of Bilad al-Sham, and equally ignored Mt. Lebanon's past as home to other confessional denominations and those ruling elites that were neither Druze nor Maronite.[4] In turn, the narrative of al-Yaziji (1801–71) influenced Tannus Shidyaq's monumental dynastic history of notable families, *Akhbar al-aʿyan fi Jabal Lubnan,* which Butrus al-Bustani edited and published in 1859.[5] There was nothing particularly nationalist *or* sectarian about the "feudal conditions" that either al-Yaziji or Tannus Shidyaq sketched for Mt. Lebanon. But their narrative enshrined the idea of Mt. Lebanon as an organic, if contested, territorial unit and "imagined principality" of Shihabi rule. What is less emphasized in this literature is that the structural and class-based seeds of the civil war of 1860 were sown during Shihabi rule.[6]

MOUNTAIN EMIRS AND MOUNTING CONFLICTS

When the Ottomans defeated the Mamluk army at Marj Dabiq, north of Aleppo, in 1516, they established their civil and military administration of Bilad al-Sham around three, later four, provincial capitals: Aleppo, Damascus, Tripoli, and Saida. Over time, the provinces were parceled out into emirates and granted to military clients in charge of tax collection. The early seventeenth century witnessed shifting alliances and rivalries over Ottoman tax concessions and in pursuit of territorial expansion. Eventually, the conniving Druze emir of the Shuf mountains, Fakhr al-Din II Ma'ani, sought military and financial assistance from Italian city-states and the Vatican to self-enrich and secede from Ottoman rule. Originally granted tax-farming rights by the Ottomans, Fakhr al-Din II developed his own tax base through recruiting hitherto reclusive Maronites as tax collectors—some of them recent converts from Shi'ism. He also wove out trade ties with Italian merchants and opened his realm to Jesuit and other Catholic missionaries. When his power grew to include the mountain and coastal areas, thereby threatening Ottoman authority, the imperial government treated him as a rebel. Following his capture and later execution in 1633, his tax concessions either reverted to old rivals, like the Harfushs of the Kisrawan district, or to smaller upstart families like the Shihabis of Wadi al-Taym. The latter would replace the Ma'anis as the major ruling house of Mt. Lebanon in the late eighteenth century.[7] Emir Bashir II al-Shihabi (1767–1850) ruled over the intricate web of kinship loyalties extending across Mt. Lebanon for over fifty years. Nominally under the authority of the Ottoman governor in Acre and later under Egypt's General Ibrahim Pasha, Bashir

II managed to shift the balance of power away from Istanbul. His rule was sustained by the wealth and power of landed families, but the financial pressures on this system grew exponentially as the Ottoman governors in Acre demanded ever-higher taxes from him only to be passed on to the peasants.

European and Ottoman rivalry deeply affected the social, political, and economic order of Mt. Lebanon before and during Bashir II's reign. The Ottoman empire was forced to make unprecedented concessions to the other European powers in the peace treaty with Russia at Küçük Kaynarca in 1774. Subsequent military incursions from Egypt strengthened the Ottoman government's commitment to local power dynasties in Acre and Damascus. Short military campaigns by Russia in Beirut (1772 and 1774) and France in Egypt (1798) and Palestine (1800–01) brought European interests in the region menacingly close. But the greatest challenge to the Shihabi regime came from peasant uprisings.[8] In 1821, thousands of predominantly Christian but also Druze commoners from the Kisrawan and Matn regions gathered north of Beirut to refuse the emir's tax demands. Squeezed between popular resistance and a hostile Ottoman governor in Saida, Emir Bashir II fled to the Hawran region. However, his rivals were unable to capitalize on Bashir's exile. Instead, the allied Jumblat forces crushed the uprising and confiscated its leaders' belongings. Bashir II was pardoned and returned to his palace in Bait al-Din.[9] Four years later, the emir had the Druze leader and erstwhile ally Bashir Jumblat killed and distributed the latter faction's lands to the Maronite church and notables, and "for the first time in the history of the Emirate, Christian officials nearly monopolized the highest political positions."[10]

During this period, the thriving silk trade in the largely Druze-populated Shuf Mountains had brought about a large-scale, southbound Maronite labor migration. Druze notables began to seek the council and scribal services of Christians. Some Druze and Muslims converted to Christianity, including members of the ruling Shihabi dynasty. In fact, until the Egyptian invasion in 1831, there was a widely tolerated and officially sanctioned confessional ambivalence.[11] Emir Bashir II's own religious affiliation depended on the context in which he found himself. European travelers to Mt. Lebanon expressed exasperation at the indeterminacy of the emir's "true belief." One British traveler complained that Bashir II had "a religion to suit the place he may be in; when he comes down to Beirut, he goes to the mosque; but in the mountain he is always a Christian."[12] The increased sectarian incitement of foreign powers coupled with the introduction of principles of equality among Ottoman subjects made such ambivalence untenable and exacerbated class and religious divisions leading up to civil strife and outright rebellion.

REFORM AND REBELLION

From 1831 to 1840, Egypt occupied Bilad al-Sham and subjected the population to a series of centralizing reforms. General Ibrahim Pasha established greater public security and opened up society and the economy to European merchant capital.[13] He also took the fateful measure of drafting Christians to suppress Druze revolts, thereby effectively turning shifting factional tensions into increasingly fixed religious enmity. While Bashir II "was a contented master in a gilded cage," the commoners felt the crunch of "taxation, conscription, disarmament, deforestation,

and corvée labour."[14] On June 8, 1840, commoners from all
denominations gathered to declare open revolt against Egyptian
rule. The meeting in Antilyas, as *Nafir Suriyya* reminded its readers, was noticeable not only for its cross-communal alliance but
also because the rebels got their leaders to speak in the name of
the people, liberty, and Ottoman legitimacy.[15]

The days of Shihabi rule were numbered when a British-
Austrian naval attack a little later in 1840 ousted the Egyptian
army and exiled the aging emir to Malta. The periodic out-
breaks of communal violence in 1841, 1844, and 1860 as well as
the Maronite peasant uprising against their Maronite landlords
of 1858–59 drew European powers into two decades of conflict
over the geographical, demographic, and administrative con-
tours of Mt. Lebanon. The Maronite patriarch, his bishops,
and French Catholic circles in particular echoed one another's
myths about the inviolable "privileges and traditions" of the
Maronite community and the historical connections—if not
"blood ties"—between the latter and the French. Many Lebanese nationalists were later to accept as a given the chimera
of Christian entitlement to Mt. Lebanon that emerged only
during this mutual mirroring between French and Maronite
Church claims.[16] At the time, the French-Maronite project faced
a number of obstacles, however. Not only did the French government subordinate it to the larger concerns of the Eastern
Question but the Maronite community itself was deeply split
over the future of Mt. Lebanon. Moreover, the Ottoman government, backed by the British, sought to integrate Mt. Lebanon
into a reorganized Bilad al-Sham and to balance the Maronites'
political ambition with support for the Druze notables, especially the returning landlords whose authority Emir Bashir II
had usurped. A battle of petitions ensued in which Ottomans

and local leaders tried to buttress their visions with representations of "popular sentiments."[17]

Conflicting claims were compounded by different interpretations of the Ottoman reform discourse that had been inaugurated by the Gülhane Decree of 1839. Partially because of the Ottoman decree's invocation of equality, Maronite commoners felt entitled to challenge the traditional authority of the Druze landlords, who in turn rejected the notion of equality and insisted on their obedience. In 1841, a seemingly innocuous dispute over hunting rights in a village near the prosperous mixed town of Dayr al-Qamar led to an attack by armed Druze men. The incident eviscerated Ma'ani and Shihabi practices of cooperation between Druze landed elites and the Maronite Church. Ottoman and European schemes to resolve this new crisis were based on the assumption that it was an outburst of primordial enmity and designed to suit the interests of these powers. The compromise outcome was the administrative reorganization of Mt. Lebanon along communal lines in 1842 and 1845, which some historians have identified as the first institutionalization of the modern phenomenon of sectarianism.[18]

The international compromise that prevailed from 1845 to 1858—the *dual qaimaqamate*—saw the northern mountain range administered by a Maronite notable, the southern mountains by a Druze notable, and the mixed districts by a representative of minority populations, under the general authority of the Ottoman governor in Saida. This complicated arrangement satisfied neither those who felt their social power eroding nor the peasants who felt emboldened by the reformist discourse of representation and started challenging the authority of their masters.

The popular uprising in the Kisrawan district of 1858–59 was the peasants' response to the *dual qaimaqamate*. Under the leadership of Tanyus Shahin, a muleteer from the village of Rayfun, hundreds of armed Maronite commoners drove the coconfessional Khazin *muqata'ji*s out of their districts and looted their residences. What distinguished this uprising from previous ones was that the rebels appropriated the Ottoman reform discourse to challenge the social hierarchy by mobilizing their faith for political purposes and against a notable family of the same faith-based community.[19] Between 1841 and 1858, then, the burgeoning idea of an autonomous Mt. Lebanon replaced the "feudal order"—still upheld by al-Yaziji and Tannus al-Shidyaq—with a new conception of social equality and political representation.

In May 1860, a few hundred rebels crossed the al-Kalb River heading south, where, they conjectured, their fellow Maronite peasants needed protection from Druze overlords. The appearance of bands of well-armed men in the mixed district of Matn inflamed an already tense situation.[20] Most scholars today agree that the skirmishes of the last week in May started the all-out civil war in Mt. Lebanon and were caused by Christian attacks on Druze villages. Within days the fighting spread to Wadi al-Taym, where seventeen Shihabi family members were hunted down and murdered, and to the Jezzin district, where fifteen hundred Christian residents were killed. Many more fled to the coastal city of Saida and to the town of Hasbaya at the foot of Mt. Hermon, where a further massacre of unarmed Christians occurred in early June. In mid-June, the city of Zahleh, in the northern Beka' Valley, fell to Druze forces.[21] On June 21, Dayr al-Qamar was sacked long after its inhabitants had surrendered and an estimated two thousand Christians were massacred.[22]

SECTARIAN ORDERS, IMPERIAL PACIFICATIONS, AND PATRIOTIC VISIONS

News of the civil war in Mt. Lebanon and Damascus traveled fast to Europe and beyond. France was quickest to respond. Paris dispatched an army of six thousand soldiers under General de Beaufort d'Hautpoul, whose mission was to punish the Druze victors and revive what Carol Hakim described as the "Franco-Lebanese dream" of Christian sovereignty. General de Beaufort adopted the Maronite clergy's position, expressed forcefully by the Bishop of Saida and Butrus al-Bustani's avuncular nemesis 'Abdallah al-Bustani (1780–1866). The latter informed Napoleon III that "the French expedition has come to Syria to protect the Christians and deliver them from oppression and tyranny."[23]

But de Beaufort had to contend with his own government, which had a more comprehensive view of the problem, as well as with the skillful Ottoman special envoy, Fu'ad Pasha, who was determined to nip European military intervention in the bud. Fu'ad Pasha's pacification policy, too, singled out the Druze leadership, including Bashir Jumblat's son, Sa'id Bey, as the main culprit, and had them hanged or exiled. Compared to Ottoman interventions of the earlier times, which the old mantra "let bygones be bygones" best exemplified, Fu'ad Pasha sought to mark a clean break with the past.[24] Significantly, he had a postwar vision for Bilad al-Sham as a whole, a vision that the young British representative on the International Commission of Inquiry, Lord Dufferin, shared when he declared that

As a general rule when you have to deal with a large population differing in their religious opinions, but perfectly assimilated in language and manners and habits of thought, the principle of fusion rather than that of separation is the one to be adopted. Religious beliefs ought not be converted into a geographical expression, and a wise government would insist upon the various subject sects subordinating their polemical to their civil relations with one another.[25]

In this immediate and urgent context, *Nafir Suriyya*'s narrative sided with Fu'ad Pasha and Lord Dufferin against the Franco-Lebanese vision in general and against Bishop 'Abdallah al-Bustani in particular. Effectively, Butrus al-Bustani called out the bishop's Maronite victimology.[26] As our translation in part 2 shows, *Nafir Suriyya* also partially adopted al-Yaziji's and Tannus Shidyaq's version of history, according to which the Druze-Maronite consensus held together the particular communal and feudal mixture of the region's time-honored system of rule. The underlying engine of this history was family factionalism, which, as al-Bustani reiterated, went back to the rivalry between northern Arabian (Qaysi) and southern Arabian (Yamani) settlement in Bilad al-Sham during the Arab conquest. al-Bustani, however, recast this condition as a liability where his predecessors saw in it an asset. He acknowledged in *Nafir Suriyya* that the civil war in 1860 was not an isolated mountain affair but affected Bilad al-Sham as a whole. As we will argue in the last chapter of part 1, the title *Nafir Suriyya* gestured toward this wider geographical context and raised the idea that it was the shared experience of civil war that bound all people in Bilad al-Sham together as "Syrians" in an affective community of "compatriots" under the sign of Ottoman sovereignty. al-Bustani's own life trajectory, to which the next chapter turns, embodied this vision with all its promises and pitfalls.

CHAPTER 2

Butrus al-Bustani

From Protestant Convert to Ottoman Patriot
and Arab Reformer

JENS HANSSEN AND HICHAM SAFIEDDINE

Butrus al-Bustani is a key figure of nineteenth-century *Nahda*.[1] Historians relied mainly on obituaries and funeral speeches to piece together what amounted to the biography of a remarkably complex and evolving thinker. The family of Butrus, son of Bulus, son of ʿAbdallah al-Bustani, hailed from the northern village of Baqr Qasha in Mt. Lebanon, situated between the coastal city of Tripoli and the highland town of Bsharré.[2] In the late eighteenth century, Butrus's grandfather moved to the confessionally mixed and economically prospering town of Dayr al-Qamar in Mt. Lebanon's Shuf Mountains. The latter sloped up from the coastal strip stretching between the Ottoman administrative center of Saida in the south and the emerging port and economic powerhouse of Beirut in the north. The grandfather then settled in nearby Dibbieh, where Butrus was later born in November 1819.[3] Around this time, Maronite peasants began to migrate south into the Shuf—which was dominated by Druze emirs and sheikhs—to look for work in the silk industry. Meanwhile, Greek Orthodox and Catholic families established minor intellectual centers in nearby Shwayfat, Kafr Shima, Shemlan, and coastal Damour.[4]

Young Butrus attended the prestigious Maronite boarding school at ʿAyn Warqa, where he studied and later taught theology, logic, and philosophy and acquired a number of classical and contemporary languages. According to George Antonius, he "stood out among his contemporaries, both for his character and for the brilliance of his attainments; and the monks selected him for a scholarship at the Maronite College in Rome. He was willing to go but his recently widowed mother wept at the thought of her son being sent so far and entreated him to stay."[5] al-Bustani left ʿAyn Warqa after the Egyptian occupation and the reign of Bashir II ended in 1840 but remained in the Saida-Dayr al-Qamar-Beirut triangle all his life.

Many of al-Bustani's future associates would leave Mt. Lebanon for the same Beirut neighborhood, the extramural Zokak al-Blat, where Protestant missionaries had set up shop. Nasif al-Yaziji left the court of the Arslan emirs at Kafr Shima in 1840. Other Nahdawis arrived in Zokak al-Blat at around the same time. Khalil al-Khuri (1836–1907), Beirut's first private newspaper owner, was the first to popularize a sense of Syrian identity.[6] Khalil Sarkis (1842–1915), an orphaned convert to Protestantism who was to apprentice at Khuri's *Hadiqat al-Akhbar*, arrived in the neighborhood as a young boy. Sarkis became al-Bustani's in-law and founded the newspaper *Lisan al-Hal*. After 1860, scholars like Husayn Bayhum (1833–81) and ʿAbd al-Qadir al-Qabbani (1847–1935) also moved to Zokak al-Blat from intramural Beirut to form scientific, literary, and educational partnerships with these Mt. Lebanon emigres.[7]

al-Bustani's descent from the Shuf Mountains to the coast was a move into exile in two senses: he left behind his home, job, and family, and he also left behind his Maronite faith.

There are conflicting stories about al-Bustani's conversion to Protestantism but the following reconstruction appears the most plausible: al-Bustani had a faith-related fallout in ʿAyn Warqa—probably with the Maronite patriarch himself. Such disagreement may, in the worst case, have resulted in excommunication and banishment, even death. To escape such a fate, he quit his job and relocated to Beirut, where Protestant missionaries had opened a chapel for preaching in Arabic the previous year.[8] al-Bustani's reputation as a "famous student from a famous school, proficient in Arabic, Syriac, knowing Latin and speaking Italian" preceded him. He was welcomed in the American mission, where, in the recollections of his friend Cornelius Van Dyck, "it was not long before he acquired the English language."[9]

The less friendly Protestant missionary Henri Jessup recalled that "about the year 1840 [al-Bustani] found, in reading the Syriac Testament, the doctrine of justification by faith, and leaving the monastic retreat, fled to Beirut, where he entered the house of Dr. Eli Smith [in Zokak al-Blat] for protection."[10] Sometime before June 1842, al-Bustani "[had] become gradually, and from his own reflections, a firm Protestant, and manifest[ed] tender conscience."[11] al-Bustani and Smith became close friends and intellectual soul mates between 1841 and Smith's death in 1857. During this period, al-Bustani learned typesetting, book printing, and oratory skills. His first major Arabic translation, *al-Bab al-maftuh fi ʿamal al-ruh* in 1843, was Eli Smith's doctrinal text of the Protestant faith. At the height of his missionary zeal, al-Bustani briefly considered the civil strife unfolding in the mid-1840s as an opportunity to proselytize, or—in his words— "an opening for the propagation of the gospel and a hastening of the approach of the day of the discomfiture of false worships." Yet, when he lost family members in a Druze raid on his village

Dibbieh in 1845, al-Bustani reportedly blamed its occurrence on irresponsible Christians who had provoked the conflict.[12]

al-Bustani's marriage to Rahil ʿAta (1826–94) was a watershed in his life. While unacknowledged in the historiography until recently, their relationship came to influence the *Nahda*'s ideals of domestic love and equality.[13] Rahil ʿAta was born to a Greek Orthodox family in Beirut. She was educated in the household of Eli and Sarah Smith (d. 1836), where she functioned as a kind of translator-companion in residence and "took a rank somewhere between a daughter and a servant."[14] She became one of the first girls at their American Mission School for Girls to learn English, and soon she began teaching there. She made a name for herself as a translator of children's books into Arabic, and by the time Rahil and Butrus met at Eli Smith's office, she was a leader in the growing community of Beirutis associated with the Protestant missionaries. Rahil hesitated to accept Butrus's marriage proposal. When she finally did in 1843, it forced her to elope because her widowed mother disapproved of the groom on account of his conversion. Although historical sources on her are silent, Rahil appears to have been an active partner in al-Bustani's translation work for the missionaries, the evangelical work for the Native Church, and his social, educational, and literary activism. She also helped set up the first of Beirut's many literary societies in late 1847.[15]

In the late 1840s, the American missionaries attempted to recruit al-Bustani to become an ordained minister.[16] As with the Maronites' attempt to send him to Rome, he was reluctant. Perhaps his zeal had worn off, or his family duties took precedence. In a letter dated January 6, 1852, al-Bustani wrote to Smith: "my present resolution is to accept no office either religious or secular that is public, for many reasons which I wish to keep to myself not wishing to be called upon to give them out."[17] Instead, he had organized the local Protestant community to petition for an Arabic-speaking Protestant church.[18] After months of resistance from missionaries, the Native Church of Beirut was founded in 1848, the year al-Bustani was recalled to Beirut to work with Eli Smith on the massive project of translating the Bible into Arabic.[19]

Two years earlier, al-Bustani had joined the most liberal-minded American missionary Cornelius van Dyck to teach at the new Protestant seminary of ʿAbayh. From there he commuted frequently back to Beirut to maintain his recent marriage and growing family.[20] Through Cornelius van Dyck's intervention, al-Bustani finally obtained financial security when he became first dragoman at the American consulate in Beirut in 1851. The position, which he held until 1862, allowed him to gain financial self-subsistence to devote his career to education, publishing, and cultural life. He cofounded multiple salons that attracted a wide multiconfessional membership.[21] al-Bustani lectured on slavery, Beirut's history, and classical Arabic poetry—topics that suggest the growing intellectual curiosity he would pursue more systematically in the 1860s and 1870s. His first publications appeared in the 1840s: he translated *The Pilgrim's Progress* in 1844; a textbook on arithmetic came out in 1848; and another on accounting three years later.[22] His famous lecture "The Education of Women," published in 1849, "intended to bring about an awakening *[nahda]* of women's determination to acquire knowledge so that they are treated with dignity, and also to rally men to support the reform of the women's dire situation and activities."[23]

al-Bustani's conversion to Protestantism was in part an escape from a Maronite clergy that had just abducted and killed' Asʿad Shidyaq, one of the first Maronite converts.[24]

As'ad Shidyaq died enchained in solitary confinement in 1830, disowned by his family and abandoned by the American missionaries, who refused to come to his defence.[25] Much later, al-Bustani "broke the Ottoman-Arab silence that had covered up the tragedy" in his manuscript *Qissat As'ad Shidyaq*. Written in early 1860, it accused the Maronite patriarch in no uncertain terms of culpability while at the same time eschewing the missionaries' sectarian narrative of the events. As Makdisi cogently argues, al-Bustani did not present a holier-than-thou version but, rather, offered "an unprecedented ecumenism, and later [in *Nafir Suriyya*] a new liberal pluralism as intolerable to American missionaries as it was to the Maronite Church."[26]

The promulgation of the Ottoman imperial reform decree—the Hatt-ı Hümayun of 1856—had an immediate and profound impact on al-Bustani.[27] What the Ottoman state offered was the opposite of what most foreign missionaries stood for. He became convinced that the Ottoman state's commitment to protecting the rights of all subjects would overcome the kind of violence and reentrenched feudal privilege that haunted Mt. Lebanon since the withdrawal of Egyptian troops. Equality between Ottoman Muslims and Christians was a noble principle that al-Bustani was willing to endorse in word and deed.[28]

The death of his friend and mentor Eli Smith, a year after al-Bustani's Ottoman turn, led him to reconsider further his relationship with the Protestant mission in Beirut. Cooperation on the Bible translation ceased. His break with the American missionaries was complete when, just before the civil war, he published his account of As'ad al-Shidyaq's conversion. Preoccupation with Arabic literature supplanted his evangelicalism. In 1859, al-Bustani delivered a long and much-referenced speech on Arab culture, its past glories, its independent formation from the rise of Islam, and its challenges in the present and future. He identified the Arabic language as the cultural unifier of diverse religious groups and "races" in Bilad al-Sham. Revival *and* innovation were indispensable for survival vis à vis the West and essential to live up to the expectations of Ottoman reform.[29]

If the Hatt-ı Hümayun of 1856 had raised al-Bustani's hopes for the possibility of creating modern foundations of society, the civil war in the summer of 1860 shook his optimism profoundly. The reckless behavior of "fanatical" Christian and Druze mountain communities not only "cost twenty thousand people their lives [and] burnt down approximately thirty thousand houses." It also jeopardized the golden opportunity that the Ottoman reform decree provided for the development of their country.[30] al-Bustani's initial reaction to the fratricidal catastrophe was to immerse himself in the urgent task of organizing the international relief effort for the thousands of refugees who had arrived in Beirut from all over Mt. Lebanon and from Damascus in the summer of 1860. But his participation in the world's first humanitarian aid operation could barely cover up the inner turmoil the civil war caused him. As he watched the mountain go up in "flames," the suffering of his former Maronite community must have affected him regardless of his conversion or the question of who cast the first stone. It was as if his compatriots were unable to handle the responsibilities that came with the rights granted by the Ottoman sultan.

AL-BUSTANI AFTER NAFIR SURIYYA

It is not entirely clear why al-Bustani stopped writing the pamphlets of *Nafir Suriyya* in April 1861. Given that the eleventh issue reads in large part like a summary of points made previously, he appears to have planned to make this his last intervention. His intention to stop writing may well have had to do with trying to reach a larger audience and having a more profound effect on society through engaging with more long-term cultural projects. Bustani articulated his first ideas for the three projects his name became most associated with in *Nafir Suriyya:* the foundation of al-Madrasa al-Wataniyya (the National School) in 1863; the publication of a series of journals in 1870, the most long-lived, innovative, and influential of which was *al-Jinan;* and his lexicographical work which started in 1867.[31]

al-Bustani declared education as the prime means to raise politically and socially responsible subjects in the ninth pamphlet of *Nafir Suriyya.* After he passed on his job as a dragoman at the American consulate general to his eldest son, Salim, he began lobbying for Ottoman permissions and local funding for the establishment of a school where he could educate a new generation of young students in the autoemancipatory and self-reflective virtues he had espoused in his writings. In September 1863, 115 boarders were admitted to his al-Madrasa al-Wataniyya—the "native Academy," as suspicious American missionaries called the building in Zuqaq al-Bulat.[32] Although some missionaries complained that the school deprived the mission of its local teaching staff, and that it was not linked to their Protestant work, William Thomson and Cornelius van Dyck—the "liberal caucus" among American missionaries—quickly realized the potential of al-Bustani's institution:

> The teachers are not allowed to impart religious instruction, but still it is an interesting fact that in a little over three years after the dreadful scenes of massacres and blood[shed] in 1860, there should be gathered in Beirut a school of 115 boarders composed of almost all the various sects in the land and that children of Moslem sheikhs and papal priests, and Druze *okkal*s should study side by side... It is a promising fact, too, as bearing upon the future success of the college proposed to be opened in Beirut that the youth of Syria are willing to pay for education, and it is plain that the movement for a college started not a moment too soon.[33]

The school was oriented toward teaching languages, Arabic, and related disciplines, such as penmanship, translation, elementary jurisprudence, land surveying, and double-entry bookkeeping, all handy subjects for the government service. The school's opening caused huge distress among the Maronite clergy and Protestant missionaries.[34] Daniel Bliss, the president of the Syrian Protestant College (now the American University of Beirut) from 1866 to 1902, continued to question the benefit and efficacy of a school that functioned as a preparatory school for his college but displayed so little missionary zeal and taught more students French than English. Efforts by the Syrian Protestant mission's board of directors to interfere with the curriculum of the National School and to impose conditions on Butrus al-Bustani ended in acrimony, and the financial and institutional ties between the two schools were severed once and for all. Daniel Bliss concluded that "we shall not consent to pay for anything we have not absolute control over."[35]

In the few student recollections that exist, the school was remembered for its tolerance and the quality of its teachers. al-Bustani recruited a dozen established literati and experienced educators for his school who shared the principle tenet that pupils should be accepted "from all sects, *millet*s, and races without discriminating against their personal beliefs or any attempt at proselytizing and [should be given] full license to carry out their religious duties."[36]

In 1867, the teachers at al-Bustani's National School were at the center of a new literary club for young thinkers. The Syrian Scientific Society constituted itself "for the spread knowledge, science, and arts."[37] With its well over one hundred members, the society was decidedly interconfessional, if not antisectarian, and had a far greater outreach than its predecessors. Most of the members were Beirutis in their early twenties, but its network spanned from Istanbul to Damascus and Cairo. The club was again presided over by al-Bustani and his neighbor and future Ottoman parliamentarian Husayn Bayhum. Lectures included topics like Syrian archaeology and Greek philosophy, translations of the works of François Guizot, and *al-tamaddun* as civilization and as Arab modernity. In its two-year existence, the society attempted to relate the past achievements of Arab civilization to modern Western science, sometimes narrated as a cultural debt owed to Arabs, sometimes as a call for reciprocity.

In the 1870s, al-Bustani expanded the reach of his ideological project by publishing what Tibawi wittily called a "horticultural trio" of journals: the monthly journal *al-Jinan* (The Gardens), *al-Janna* (Paradise), and *al-Junayna* (Little Garden).[38] On the first page of its inaugural issue of *al-Jinan*, al-Bustani lays down his mission: *al-Jinan* wishes to "open the gates to the gardens of knowledge and a space where the pens of the intellectuals . . . invite participation of elites and commoners in the circulation of ideas and knowledge."[39] Paradise and garden, of course, share genealogical communalities. Both the Quran and the Bible describe paradise as a garden. But not all gardens represented the afterlife or were cosmic.[40] The semantic recurrence of the garden/gardener in the *Nahda* (not just in Beirut but also in Istanbul, Cairo, and Baghdad) indexed a deeper discursive practice, a "botanical imagination" at the center of the collective effort to "curate" an ideal/Edenic political space and community. In fact, between 1858 and 1900 dozens of Arabic newspapers across the Arab provinces of the Ottoman empire invoked the garden in one way or another.

al-Jinan, in particular, was a laboratory of social reform, self-criticism, and cultural revival for the growing numbers of learned men and women in fin de siècle Beirut. Its serialized historical novels and editorials were public opinion–shaping journalistic events around an urban network of correspondents and readers in the Arabic-speaking Ottoman empire and North Africa. Beirut's cultural production capitalized on an unprecedented global demand for Mt. Lebanon's silk between the 1860s and the 1880s.[41] Both fields of production, sericulture and serialized novels published in journals, were economic and affective wagers on the future. Like al-Bustani's most remarkable intellectual feats—the Arabic lexicon, *Muhit al-Muhit,* and his epic work on the Arabic encyclopaedia, the multitomed *Daʾirat al-Maʿarif*—*al-Jinan* would have been financially inconceivable without the economic optimism of the 1860s, reliant, as all projects were, on advance subscriptions by Arabic readers.[42]

al-Bustani's reinvention as an encyclopaedist marks a wider shift in the *Nahda. Nafir Suriyya* was an urgent and immediate address to al-Bustani's contemporaries and *al-Jinan*'s editorials no less impatiently repeatedly told its readers to swallow the bitter pill of self-reliance and autoemancipation. The lexicographical project in the autumn of his life, however, operated on a different horizon of expectation and a much more long-term frame of reform. Removed from the immediate concerns of social cohesion that had so animated *Nafir Suriyya,* al-Bustani was set on erecting a monument of modern Arabic philology for future generations. As he declared in the introduction to *Muhit al-Muhit,* he also saw his lexicon as an attempt to decenter "the Arabian Desert as the *terra prima* of Arabo-Islamic civilization."[43] What was at stake in al-Bustani's project was achieving Arab culture, literally word for word, in order to stem the perceived loss of "pure Arabic" as much as to incorporate its Syriac and other Shami etymological legacies. This was all the more urgent because, as Ahmad Faris al-Shidyaq intoned in his *al-Saq 'ala al-saq* in 1855, "While the Europeans have acquired their language from civilization, we have acquired our civilization from our language."[44]

After 1860, al-Bustani saw his task as reconsidering that civilization critically. Before we consider some key concepts in *Nafir Suriyya* and situate the claims about language and civilization in chapter 5, the next chapter will provide a sketch of the place of *Nafir Suriyya* in modern Arab historiography.

CHAPTER 3

Nafir Suriyya in Arab Historiography

JENS HANSSEN

Early Arabic historiography of the *Nahda* focused largely on al-Bustani as a pioneer of the Arab language reform and revival movement and paid more attention to his literary and scientific output than the less polished and more political *Nafir Suriyya*.[1] The latter's pamphlet format has also made it an outlier in the historiography on early Arabic newspapers and journalism. But Arabic- and European-language literature did recognize the importance of *Nafir Suriyya*. Its interpretation has shifted over the course of the twentieth century. George Antonius's foundational study-turned-manifesto of Arab nationalism identified the pamphlets as the "the first germ of the national idea" in Syria:

> It was a small weekly *[sic]* publication called *The Clarion of Syria,* the first political journal ever published in the country, and was mainly devoted to the preaching of concord between the different creeds and union in the pursuit of knowledge. For knowledge, he argued week after week in the earnest columns of his paper, leads to enlightenment; and enlightenment, to the death of fanaticism and the birth of ideals held in common. A platitude perhaps, but one that Syria had not heard before, and which contained the germ of the national idea.[2]

Albert Hourani echoed Antonius's patriotic sentiments but insisted that al-Bustani "writes as an Ottoman subject, and there is no hint that he would wish to break away from loyalty to the sultan." Instead, "his appeal is to those who belong to a smaller unit within the empire and, as with [the Egyptian reformer] Tahtawi, the unit is a territorial one." In Hourani's interpretation, "'Syria' as a whole is his *watan*" and al-Bustani "is perhaps the first writer to speak of 'Arab blood.' If Syria was to flourish again, they must love her, and, what is no less urgent, they must be on friendly terms with each other." Compared to other mid-nineteenth-century Arab intellectual giants, "al-Bustani lays his emphasis on religious freedom and equality, and mutual respect between those of different faiths." Hourani explains this move with al-Bustani's Protestant conversion, which he saw as a form of "self-exile [that] may well have turned his mind to the thought of some wider community to which he could belong." al-Bustani distinguished "between two different types of religion: between the fanaticism *(ta'assub)* which has ruined Syria, and the mutual respect between faiths which should exist and did once exist." Finally, Hourani invokes al-Bustani's belief in the emancipatory potential of civilization: "If Syria is to be truly civilized, she needs two things from her rulers: just and equal laws suited to the times, looking to the matter at issue and not to the person, and based on a separation between religious and secular realms; and education in Arabic. Syria must not become a Babel of languages as she is a Babel of religions."[3]

al-Bustani confessed how difficult it was to find the right words, language, and narrative to represent adequately what happened during the civil war and what it meant for the future. While his *Khutba* of 1859 and his *Khitab* of 1868 were originally delivered as scholarly lectures and retained the assertive style of a religious sermon in published versions, *Nafir Suriyya* cast spells of doubt and constantly gestured toward the unknown and the conditionality of its truth claims.[4] He categorized and divided the world into conceptual opposites—past/present, religion/politics, civilization/barbarism, Europe/Africa, victims/perpetrators, civil war/civil society. He separated the financial from the moral-cultural losses *(al-khasa'ir al-adabiyya)*, and then all the losses from the potential gains. What may come across as the work of an accountant's balance sheet is in fact part of al-Bustani's broader approach to try to master, by way of simplification, infinitely complex situations.[5]

Most historians of the Middle East have judged *Nafir Suriyya*'s invocation of *al-watan*—patriotism—as articulating a protean form of twentieth-century Arab nationalisms. For some, since George Antonius and Albert Hourani, it was the source of progress and independence, while for its detractors it unleashed the destruction of an authentic political order where everyone had known their place.

Hourani's Palestinian contemporaries Abdulatif Tibawi and Hisham Sharabi largely shared his interpretation of *Nafir Suriyya* as the work of an anguished Christian Arab of the modernizing Ottoman empire. An early historian of American missionaries in the Arab world, Tibawi noticed al-Bustani's support for the Ottoman envoy Fu'ad Pasha's pacifying mission and argued that it was rooted in his "conflicting loyalties" to his former Maronite coreligionists in Mt. Lebanon, on the one hand, and the new Protestant and American community he served in Beirut, on the other. Although Tibawi demonstrated that al-Bustani had become somewhat estranged from the American mission by 1860, he still considered *Nafir Suriyya*'s "gospel" style the product of his evangelical milieu, living among American missionaries.[6] Sharabi, a Palestinian-American political scientist who had been an early member of the Syrian Socialist Nationalist Party, focused on *Nafir Suriyya* as an expression of Christian secularism and emergent Syrian nationalism, and the unifying purpose of the Arabic language as "a common ground where Christian and Muslim could meet."[7]

Hourani's student, the late Butrus Abu-Manneh argued in his seminal study from 1980 on al-Bustani's identitarian disposition that the promise of Ottoman liberal reform, religious equality, and participatory rule enshrined in the Hatt-ı Hümayun of 1856 "converted" him once more, this time to Ottomanism. The Ottoman reform decree convinced al-Bustani that the Ottoman state was the most reliable guarantor of bringing about a modern social order in Bilad al-Sham. Like his Palestinian colleagues Tibawi and Sharabi, Abu Manneh identified historical Syria, not Lebanon, as the cultural and national referent: "al-Bustani led the way culturally to Arabism, politically to Ottomanism, and inevitably to Syrian nationalism."[8]

Following Lebanon's descent into politically motivated sectarian violence during the 1970s and 1980s, some historians reclaimed al-Bustani as a Lebanese patriot against the then dominant Syrianist appropriation.[9] For the Arabic editor of *Nafir Suriyya,* Yusuf Quzma Khuri, al-Bustani was a "man before his age" who provided contemporary Lebanon with a blueprint for overcoming civil war.[10] In the work of Ussama Makdisi, al-Bustani and his *Nafir Suriyya* came to be recalibrated in the distinctly Lebanese context of coping with communal violence. Makdisi's work combines Tibawi's critique of the impact of missionaries on the *Nahda* with Abu Manneh's interest in al-Bustani's Ottomanism.[11] But according to Makdisi, the real lesson contained in al-Bustani's post-1860 thought was for Lebanon to learn: "al-Bustani asserted that the mixture of religion and politics would lead to an inflexible political system that could not adapt to new realities, anticipating almost word for word modern-day criticisms of the sectarian political system that dominates Lebanon."[12]

In the aftermath of Syria's descent into civil war and the harrowing refugee crisis today, *Nafir Suriyya*'s frame of reference reminds us that sectarian violence is not an isolated Lebanese phenomenon. al-Bustani himself alluded to the wider afflictions that had struck Aleppo in 1850, Nablus in 1856, and Damascus in 1860.[13] Indeed, the massacre of Christians in Bab Tuma—many of them refugees from Mt. Lebanon—had two contradictory effects. On the one hand, neither the Ottoman nor the European governments could treat the civil war in Mt. Lebanon in isolation from Bilad al-Sham as a whole. On the other hand, the massacres in Damascus reinforced Maronite claims of more general Muslim hostility against Christians. As Carol Hakim has pointed out, "the Damascus massacres obscured the specific political and socioeconomic factors of the outbreak of hostilities in Lebanon and vindicated the view attributing them exclusively to the baleful designs of an inflamed Muslim fanaticism."[14] In this sense, *Nafir Suriyya*'s wider Bilad al-Sham lens designated not so much a modern—much less an ancient—possessive territorial framework for the "Syrian nation" as the source of attachment (what *Nafir Suriyya* refers to as "*'illat al-dhamm*")[15] whose members needed to band together and exchange violent strife with love for the homeland.

Since Makdisi's important interventions, sectarianism, nationalism, and secularism no longer appear in English historiography as conceptual rivals or stages of historical development but as dialectically conditioning one another under the sign of colonial modernity. Makdisi defines *sectarianism* as "a process through which a kind of religious identity is politicized, even

secularized, as part of a . . . struggle for power."[16] He subjected
Ottoman pacification of provincial protests and insurrections to
a colonial discourse analysis and coined the concept of "Ottoman Orientalism."[17] Makdisi's rereading of *Nafir Suriyya* con-
trasts al-Bustani's understanding of the civil war in 1860 in Mt.
Lebanon and his vision of "future's past" to those of the Ottoman special envoy Fu'ad Pasha. There were competing political
agendas between al-Bustani's advocacy of citizenship and the
authoritarian Ottomanism of Fu'ad Pasha at play:

> Despite their advocacy of Syrian patriotism and Ottoman nationalism,
> respectively, both interpreted and judged within fundamentally 19th
> century notions of progress. In other words, they both explicitly resisted
> European imperialism at the same time that they deployed a discourse
> of national and tribal time, which was itself based on European colonial-
> ist thinking that divided the world into advanced and backward nations,
> peoples, and tribes. . . . [al-Bustani] anticipated a question central to
> non-Western historiography: is it possible to represent an indigenous
> national past using a decidedly Eurocentric notion of modernity?[18]

Most recently, Makdisi argued that al-Bustani's Arab civilizing
discourse and his notion of freedom of consciousness was
inspired by Protestant ethics and Christian salvific traditions.
al-Bustani challenged both the American missionaries' exclu-
sionary and deeply racist conceptions of Protestant cultural
superiority and the homegrown sense of sectarian supremacy
espoused by the Maronite clergy. Against such intolerance, *Nafir
Suriyya* stood out for the way it charted a modern path of hybrid
identity, equality, and coexistence that allowed for "multiple
forms of religiosity."[19]

Stephen Sheehi, by contrast, reads *Nafir Suriyya* as an illus-
tration of the literary and rhetorical construction of modern
Arab identity. The framework of critical *Nahda* studies Sheehi

established enabled him to take al-Bustani and his *Nafir Suriyya* out of the Syro-Lebanese geographic and discursive confines and bring both into conversation with intellectual production in Egypt and the wider Arabic-speaking world. Sheehi is critical of al-Bustani's writings that he regards as manifestations of the *Nahda*'s bourgeois sensibilities. Frequently, the social and cultural critique al-Bustani offered his compatriots bore the hallmarks of internalized Orientalism and self-colonization. But a respectfully close, Bakhtinian reading of al-Bustani's three most important reform texts—*Khutba fi adab al-'Arab* (1859), *Nafir Suriyya,* and *Khitab fi al-hay'a al-ijtima'iyya* (1868)—reveal his and other Nahdawis' double consciousness,[20] the desire to be recognized by the West as equal and coeval on the one hand and a desire to be essentially, indeed, authentically, different.

While al-Bustani's *Khutba* idealized the Arabic literary past, and his later *Khitab* were delivered as assertive sermons that measured Arab culture against the ideal of the West, *Nafir Suriyya*'s probing exhortative style and direct appeal to "native sons" and "fellow countrymen" of "Syria" represented an incitement to subjective and individual reform among its readers. *Nafir Suriyya*'s rhetoric distinguished between two groups of "compatriots," enlightened or reformable selves and ignorant and fanatical ones. But this gulf was not absolute; it could be overcome if the latter returned to the fold through love and forgiveness for the greater good of political unity and social concord.[21] By highlighting the text's affective registers, Sheehi presents al-Bustani's civilizing project as a tentative and fragile process of nationalism. al-Bustani's vocabulary of social analysis—contagion, anxiety, and barbarism—certainly casts him as a liberal thinker, but not as a heroic, visionary intellectual pioneer. Rather he appears as someone driven by fear of social transgression and by bourgeois intolerance of subaltern mobilization.[22]

Nafir Suriyya continues to animate debates about the origins of Arab nationalism. Most recently, Nadia Bou Ali has read the civil war in 1860 as a disruption that "the forces of capitalism and the shifting relations of production in Levantine society induced," before positing *Nafir Suriyya* as an affective response for coping with the socioeconomic fallout. According to this interpretation, al-Bustani read the civil war as a manifestation of cultural atavism that deprived hardworking individuals of their rewards and civil society of its promise. al-Bustani's translation-adaptation of Daniel Defoe's *Robinson Crusoe,* which he published in 1861, has received considerable scholarly attention recently to serve as a key for a new understanding of al-Bustani's postwar reform project.[23] While for Maya Kesrouany, al-Bustani's version of *Robinson Crusoe* offers insights into the relationship between Lebanese nationalism and the *Nahda*'s translation movement, for Bou Ali al-Bustani's *Crusoe* offered a capitalist work ethic that modeled the feeling of guilt and sense of morality of every compatriot on the feats of the novel's shipwrecked protagonist.[24] Bou Ali argued that "the trope of crisis is the founding and foundational episteme of the nation form for the Arabs."[25] If al-Bustani conceived the nation form through an act of translation, it is borne out of a postwar state of emergency in which "the liberal subject is construed on a splitting between a demonized self and an innocent 'we.'"[26]

Elizabeth Holt has recently picked up the idea of a capitalism-induced cultural crisis in her monograph *Fictitious Capital: Silk, Cotton and the Rise of the Arabic Novel.* Drawing on Fawaz (1983), Labaki (1984), Khater (2001), Hanssen (2005b), and Kornbluh (2013), she argues that the emergence of the serialized Arabic novel on the pages of the Bustanis' newspapers contains literary representations—in content and form—of economic developments in Beirut, Mt. Lebanon, and Bilad al-Sham. The Ottoman-European free trade agreements between 1838 and 1840 set the stage for the influx of European commodities and capital. The silk trade took off in earnest when French investors industrialized Lebanese sericulture in the aftermath of the 1860 civil war of 1860. Capital was accumulating in the 1860s in Beirut, benefiting international but also local financiers.[27] She insists, however, that the 1860s were a period of cultural optimism. The literary expressions of crisis only set in with the economic downturn in the 1870s:

> By the early summer of 1870, . . . hopeful plotlines were undermined by the suspense charted not only at the level of form, each serialized installment ever asking readers to wait: the remainder was yet to come, but also by the historical conjuncture, a moment when the very unruliness of global—here especially French—capital was profiting at a quickening pace off the risks entailed in financing and speculating in silk moths and mulberry orchards.[28]

In *Iterations of Loss: Mutilation and Aesthetic Form, al-Shidyaq to Darwish* Jeffrey Sacks explores the destructive character of the *Nahda*'s attempt to find an adequate language, to institutionalize Arabic literature, and to adapt Arabic philology in order to meet the political, economic, juridical, and cultural challenges of colonial modernity.[29] Under the slogan of "Awake ye Arabs Awake," Nahdawis assumed the role of guardians of the Arab future.[30] But with some few exceptions, like al-Bustani's nemesis, Ahmad Faris al-Shidyaq (1804–87), they struggled with the sense of loss. The textual and architectural ruins of past grandeur all around, they asked themselves, where are we today, and what have we missed during our "ignorance" and "slumber" all these centuries? al-Bustani's writings offered a "simplified" Arabic language that could curate, in anthropocentric fashion, the once-glorious past, capture the ominous signs of the present, and project a better, albeit uncertain, future. And yet, with this ability came the mournful realization that "man's" philological mastery reduced Arabic to serving human utility and to curtailing "the iterative dimensions of language, which give language to exceed both itself and its time."[31]

CHAPTER 4

Toward a Conceptual History
of *Nafir Suriyya*

JENS HANSSEN

Both words of the title of al-Bustani's pamphlets require inves-
tigation, as well as his definition of them as *wataniyyat*: What did
he mean by *nafir* and what would have been its connotations?
And what did *Suriyya* mean to al-Bustani and his generation?
Was it a description of a real territory or a potentiality? *al-Nafir*
and *Suriyya* are terms that go back to antiquity, but neither had
much traction outside liturgical literature until contact with
Protestant missionaries gave them new political valence.

al-Nafir means "clarion" or "trumpet," which was perhaps
so self-evident that al-Bustani did not explain the term in his
pamphlets.[1] But in *Muhit al-Muhit,* he dedicated almost an entire
page to the different declinations and meanings of the root *n-f-r*
(from the "bolting of a mare," to "raising of troops," "the fugitive," "estrangement," and "mutual aversion"), before defining *al-nafir* itself: "someone enlisted in a group or cause," and
"*al-nafir al-'am*" means mass mobilization to combat the enemy."
The Protestant convert al-Bustani also lists *yawm al-nafir*
(Judgment Day)[2] and informs the reader that *al-nafir* is also a
trumpet or fanfare *(al-buq)*[3] containing associations with Israfil,

the archangel of death alluded to in the Bible and the Quran.[4] Then he mentions *Nafir Suriyya* itself as a set of "meditations on the events of 1860 published in eleven issues that we called *wataniyyat*." Like many historians before us, we translate the term as "clarion" in order to capture both the apocalyptic mood of the text and the author's passionate call for social concord and overcoming adversity.[5]

At first sight, the term *Suriyya* is less complex. After all, al-Bustani defined the territory as Barr al-Sham and Arabistan, two Ottoman terms for what later Syrian nationalists considered Greater Syria. But al-Bustani did not give clear boundaries for this land except to lament in issue 5 that "Syria lies between two countries [Egypt and Turkey] that have often pulled it in different directions." So why did he replace Barr, or Bilad al-Sham, the common referent for Ottoman Syria, with the ancient Hebrew and Latinate term *Syria*?[6] In his *Khutba* of 1859, he had delineated the essence of and threats to Arab culture, but he made no reference to Syria. *Nafir Suriyya* was the first instance where al-Bustani annunciated "ancient Syria" as a parameter of identity, as a benchmark for contemporary Syrians and a source of social unity.[7]

The political semantics first began to shift from Bilad—or Barr—al-Sham and Arabistan to Syria during the Egyptian occupation from 1831 to 1840.[8] *Nafir Suriyya*'s paradigmatic adoption of "Suriyya" very likely stems from its author's contact with American missionaries, particularly Eli Smith. In 1833, the same year Nasif al-Yaziji wrote his *Historical Treatise on the Conditions of Mount Lebanon in Its Feudal Age*, Smith had defined Syria as the "general name for the country that lies along the whole breadth of the Eastern end of the Mediterranean Sea, extending inland to the deserts of Arabia, and having the territories of Egypt on the south, and the river Euphrates with the mountains of Cilicia on the north."⁹ From the first literary society al-Bustani cofounded with Eli Smith in 1847 to Daniel Bliss's Syrian Protestant College in 1866, the Americans propagated a Syrianist imagination that was conspicuously at odds with Muslim, Ottoman, and Lebanist geographical imaginations.

Nafir Suriyya contained many ideas about Syria that were already expressed in Beirut's first privately run newspaper, *Hadiqat al-Akhbar.* Its editor-in-chief, Khalil Khuri (1836–1907), was al-Bustani's neighbor, a noted fiction writer, and an amateur historian.¹⁰ His book *Kharabat Suriyya, the Ruins of Syria* (1861) was the first in Arabic to use Syria in the title of a major *Nahda* publication and drew on archaeological texts of the early missionaries and adopted their mournfulness about current day Syria: "Where are the temples of Baalbak and Jerusalem? Where is the royal purple of Tyre? Where are the workshops of Saida and the academies of Beirut? . . . All is long gone."¹¹ The missionaries had set out to reclaim the Holy Land but instead of returning to the roots of Christianity, they ended up in Beirut, where contact with its inhabitants, particularly the literary figures, and the civil war of 1860 forced them to adjust their preconceived ideas.¹² One of *Nafir Suriyya*'s remarkable features was how it turned the experience of violence and loss—without diminishing it—into a calling for hope that even American missionaries came around to adopting. It is in this sense of forging a Syrian community of suffering that the idea of patriotism with all its contradictions— "it repeats the event it wishes only to have described"—was born.¹³

Subsequent local historians of the "Syrian nation," starting with Elias Matar (1874), Jurji Yanni (1881), and Yusuf Dibs (1893–1905), elided "Syria's" "baptism of fire" of 1860 and telescoped deep into the past.¹⁴ Like Khuri and al-Bustani, they did so relying largely on European literature.¹⁵ What changed was the emergence of geographical determinism. It had its origins in French cartography and archaeology, particularly Elisée Reclus's influential *Nouvelle géographie universelle* (1884) and Victor Bérad's *Les Phéniciens et l'Odysée* (1902), and was popularized in Beirut by the Jesuit geographer and historian Henri Lammens (1862–1937). The geographical determinism of these geographers and their students at the Université de St. Joseph was Islamophobic and anti-Ottoman. It conjured up Syria as a distinctly Christian and non-Arab territorial entity in which "Lebanon is for Syria what the Nile River is for Egypt."[16] These early expressions of Syrianism and Lebanism had much in common with each other but little with those of the Bustanis. These exclusivist ideas were an anathema to the pre-Mandate *Nahda*.

Only when the Ottoman decentralization movement and Arab nationalism challenged both Phoenicianism and the Syrian antiquity narrative after the Young Turk Revolution of 1908 did Syrian and Lebanese nationalisms start to move apart and compete with each other.[17] Syrian nationalists challenged the old narrative that Syrians were Christian. They insisted that Syrians were Arabs and began to claim that Damascus was "the beating heart of Arabism." Since the political turbulence following the end of Ottoman rule, most articulations and explorations of Arab nationalisms have focused on their transformation from "birth" to maturation to aberration, apogee, or "death." This diachronic scheme charts the transition from territory-based patriotism to ethnocentric nationalism, i.e., from nineteenth-century *wataniyya* to twentieth-century *qawmiyya*. If *al-qawmiyya* came to challenge the colonial division of the Arab nation in the twentieth century, it also criticized the alleged parochialism of *wataniyya* formations.[18] These later conceptual battles were not al-Bustani's problem space. His idea of

Syria was unencumbered by colonial and nationalist occupation with the geographic form of the nation, border drawing, and demographic exclusions. Rather, he was preoccupied with the constitution of a transcendent harmonious community.

al-Watan was the central concept throughout *Nafir Suriyya.* But in *Clarion 5*, a new sociological concept appeared for the first time, *al-jinsiyya:* the new "the source of attachment . . . is kinship *(al-jinsiyya).*" In this passage, al-Bustani laments the way in which the resurgence of prejudice *(al-gharadh)* against other groups has shifted from an interfactional designation of us versus them to one based on hitherto "sacred names, . . . like Druze and Christian, then Muslim and Christian." *al-Jinsiyya* has come to mean nationality and the normative source of attachment to the independent nation-state. al-Bustani's *al-Jinan,* Ahmad Faris al-Shidyaq's *al-Jawa'ib,* and other journals that cropped up from the 1870s onward first willed the semantic shift from kinship to nationality.[19] They understood that language can formulate new political communities.

al-Jinsiyya, an abstract noun derived from *al-jins,* occupies center stage in *Nafir Suriyya* starting from the November 1860 *Clarion,* notably when the discussion shifts from Syria to Arab culture: "we advise you to avoid this natural inclination to condemn an entire race *[al-jins]* and to attack it because of the failings of some of its members." *al-Jins,* too, has undergone significant shifts in meaning since al-Bustani penned *Nafir Suriyya.*[20] The abstract noun of *janasa* (to make alike, to classify, to assimilate), *al-jins* has been around since early Arabic literature. But in the context of racial stereotyping, it was of recent coinage, and al-Bustani may have been alerted by American missionaries' discourse on the Arabs. For example, Eli Smith invoked *al-jins al-'arabi* in a lecture to one of al-Bustani's new cultural societies in 1849. The fact that al-Bustani speaks of a "*natural* inclination" suggests that *jins* may not have referred to a new concept imported by foreigners but was likely a new term for an existing concept.

Nahdawis and missionaries alike believed that people could escape racial stereotypes. The particularly brutal history of racism in the Americas along with insights of the twentieth century spawned anticolonial theorists and critical race theorists. al-Bustani, by contrast, did not have the vocabulary to challenge racism itself. So, instead of challenging the epistemic Eurocentrism of his times, he advocated a program to improve the destiny of Arab society and individuals and adapt to new conditions. The concepts central to this undertaking were *al-adab* and *al-tamaddun.*

Today's Arabic readers know *adab* as "literature."[21] In classical Arabic *al-adab*'s semantic range included sophisticated habits, good behavior, and the ability to fulfill one's role in society, a sense it retains today negatively in the phrase *qalil al-adab* (uncouth) and positively in *mu'addab* (polite). In al-Bustani's times, *al-adab* was located somewhere between morals *(al-akhlaq)* and education *(al-ta'lim).* The former had ethical resonances in Islamic political philosophy while the latter denoted the *Nahda*'s mantra of public education, expressed by al-Bustani in his lecture "On the Education of Women," written in 1849. Neither alternative term appears in *Nafir Suriyya*—al-Bustani used *akhlaq* only once, in his follow-up article "Patriotism is an Element of Faith" in *al-Jinan,* published in 1870. In his lecture on *ādāb al-'Arab,* published in 1859, al-Bustani gestured toward the academic concept of the "Arab humanities" in the plural of *al-adab*—"the subject is *ādāb al-'Arab,* or the sciences *(al-'ulum),* arts *(al-funun),* or knowledge *(al-ma'arif)* of the Arabs."[22] But most translations, correctly, render the title as "the culture of the Arabs."[23] In *Nafir Suriyya* the meaning of *al-adab* is some-

what different from that in his lecture a year before; the emphasis is more on lessons learned from the mistakes of belligerent
human behavior and collective "unbridled passions." In this
context, *moral* and *morals* seem to have a more apt connotation
in our translation of *al-adab/adabi* than the semantics of *culture*
and *cultural*.[24]

al-Bustani dedicated issue II of *Nafir Suriyya* to the desirability
and acquirability of civilization.[25] In this final patriotic pamphlet,
al-Bustani sets out to differentiate the population, between those
who merit the homeland and the reforms he advocated, on the
one hand, and those who disqualify themselves by their unworthy deeds, on the other. Drawing on Ibn Khaldun, he claims that
al-tamaddun (civilization) is derived from the word *madina* (city)
and "opposed to the lifestyle of the Bedouins who lack civilization." "The natural state into which man is born is barrenness"
but with innovation, hard work, and diligence one can achieve
the highest standards of civilization. In many ways, al-Bustani
shared Matthew Arnold's conservative, if not elitist, definition
of culture as "the study of harmonious human perfection."[26]

Adopting the racist taxonomy of Western missionaries, al-
Bustani holds that half way between the "cannibals of distant
Africa" and the "dignitaries of Paris and England," the fault line
between barbarity and civilization passes right through Syria
between "the Arab inhabitants of the desert and the inhabitants of Beirut." But "genuine civilization is that state of social
organization which suits the development of all forces of the
human race, individually and collectively." If everybody was to
be brought into the national fold and given the chance at civilization, the prospective nation would be a distinctly urban utopia. Stereotypical Arab Bedouins, however, remain a constant
menace and anxiety-inducing threats of civilizational relapse.

Culture-talk and clash-of-civilization narratives have haunted the West and the Middle East since civilization first entered the Orientalist paradigm in the early nineteenth century.[27] But, as Peter Hill reminds us, the Arab discourse on civilization changed even during al-Bustani's lifetime. In fact, there was a significant shift between Khalil Khuri's use of *tamaddun* in the late 1850s and the invocations in *Nafir Suriyya* that reflects an intellectual crisis of confidence in al-Bustani, precipitated by the war of 1860. While the owner of *Hadiqat al-Akhbar* expressed optimism for the "new age" and autogenetic attainability of the highest stages of "civilization," the author of the "Lecture on the Culture of the Arabs" and *Nafir Suriyya* was not so sanguine about the prospects of cultural refinement alone and insisted that in the current global competitiveness, no culture is an island. By the 1870s the meaning of being a civilized compatriot had consolidated around the mastery of synthesis of essential Arab qualities and contingent European accomplishments.[28]

CHAPTER 5

Wataniyya as Antidote to Sectarianism

JENS HANSSEN

Come let us join together, O brothers
By commitment and faith allied to one another
Giving ourselves, our devotion to show,
So rise oh heroes! To the battle now go . . .
Love of birthplaces *[al-awtan]* is an article of faith.

—al-Tahtawi, *Wataniyyat,* 1855[1]

When the Orientalist Bernard Lewis lamented that the word *watan*—though apparently inferior to European and Islamic cognates like *la patrie* and *Vaterland, al-umma* and *al-milla*—had helped destroy "the universal Islamic monarchy of the Turkish sultans," his Ottoman nostalgia meant to dismiss the "patchwork quilt of *soi-disant* nation-states" that gained independence in the mid-twentieth century.[2] What interests us, by contrast, is how national historians sought to convince their own emergent constituencies that geographically ill-defined terms mattered and corresponded to distinct territories of belonging and attachment. For if "Syria" and "Lebanon" became imaginable national territories in the twentieth century, it was not because Europeans invented them. From the perspective of conceptual

history, the term that came to challenge religious visions of
colonial and imperial rule was *al-watan.*

Hindsight has given at once too much and too little credit
to al-Bustani's conceptual innovations.[3] al-Bustani's particular
use of language and history in *Nafir Suriyya* was triggered by the
event of the civil war. For him the issue was less to determine the
(Christian) essence and cultural ownership of Syria, as francophone scholars associated with the Jesuits in Beirut did. Rather
al-Bustani championed a transconfessional contract where all of
Syria's religious communities were equal before Ottoman law,
everyone felt included but also knew their place. It was in this
context that he decided to dust off the term *al-watan*—"the most
pleasant derivative word adorning the Arabic language"—in
favor of available, but by now differently connoted, alternatives.[4]
By choosing *watan* al-Bustani effectively avoided what Koselleck
called in the European context "the diachronic semantic thrust
of theological" alternatives and steered his ecumenical messian-
ism toward love of the homeland.[5] Conversely, only the nation
form would enable ecumenical religiosity. Invested with new
political meaning, particularly in relation to the forces that he
posited had given rise to the civil war (forces that only much
later acquire the seemingly stable label of "sectarianism"), the
introduction of *al-watan* and the attachment to it, *hubb al-watan,*
then was a conscious political act with a view to set the agenda
for how the event should be interpreted and how to frame the
future of his afflicted society.

Prior to the civil war in 1860, *al-watan* had already undergone significant semantic transformation. *al-watan* had traveled
from al-Jahiz's (d. 869) famous, if contested, treatise *al-Hanin ila
al-awtan* (Longing for one's homelands) to the great dictionaries of Ibn Manzur (d. 1311–12), to *Lisan al-'Arab,* and to Murtada
al-Zabidi's *Taj al-'Arus* (1770s–80s).[6] These and other instances

awtan (pl. of *watan*) implied one's home, the place of birth or residence. Ottoman sultans and Persian shahs may have deployed the term to belittle their rivals or regional insurgencies.[7] But the term did not feature in the Circle of Justice or any of the Advice to the Prince literature.[8]

Ottoman diplomats stationed in Paris during the French Revolution experimented with translating the republican slogan *patrie* but were reluctant to endorse it given the threat such concepts posed to their young sultan.[9] If the choice of translation fell on *vatan,* it may have still had the earlier negative connotations of the enemy's parochialism. But when foreign minister and former Ottoman ambassador to Paris, Mustafa Reşid Pasha (1800–1858), famously announced that the state henceforth would "guarantee insuring to our subjects perfect security for life, honor, and fortune" in the Gülhane Reform Edict of 1839, he also called upon all Ottomans to help "defend the *vatan.*"[10] This inaugural event of the Tanzimat, then, deployed the term much like al-Bustani would in *Nafir Suriyya:* as an ennobling concept of attachment and a political field of rights and duties.

Rifʿat al-Rifaʿi al-Tahtawi (1801–73) was more attracted to the July 1830 Revolution in general and the patriotism it espoused in particular than the Ottoman eyewitnesses of the French Revolution had been in Paris in the 1790s.[11] Having spent 1826 to 1831 in France, he chronicled the overthrow of the Bourbon monarchy and diligently translated the new French Constitutional Charter, including most elements of the Declaration of the Rights of Man and Citizen of 1789.[12] At a time when his patron, the ruler of Egypt Mehmed Ali Pasha, began challenging the authority of the Ottoman sultan, culminating in his military campaign in Bilad al-Sham, al-Tahtawi could imbue his writings with a critique of the injustices of the Bourbon Restoration and the excesses of monarchical rule more generally.

Geopolitics aside, the sense of cultural recovery and political reclamation that undergirded the writings and translations by *Nahda* figures like al-Tahtawi and al-Bustani also predisposed them to the spirit of the rights of man, social justice, and freedom of conscience expressed in the French Revolution.[13]

The Egyptian's *wataniyya* quotation at the beginning of this chapter suggests a kind of law of nature that required no further elaboration as to why and how this patriotic love works to be part of—much less an enactment of—faith, or, indeed, *the* faith. For all his appropriations of French Enlightenment thought, al-Tahtawi did not develop the concept of *hubb al-watan* until his late works.[14] By this time he had developed neo-Platonic and Hobbesian ideas of the state as the embodiment of the *watan,* a human organism in which the head represents the sovereign, the organs the government, and the limbs the military. While for al-Tahtawi Egypt's territoriality appeared as a fact of natural history, the function of the Arabic language was to raise faith in the modern state.[15]

Arguably, the relationship between territoriality, the state, and the Arabic language was far more fraught in *Nafir Suriyya* than in al-Tahtawi's writings, and it is to al-Bustani's credit that he openly grappled with these tensions. al-Bustani addressed his readers as *abnaʾ al-watan*—compatriots—which we render as "countrymen" in our translation, and signed each of the eleven issues of *Nafir Suriyya* anonymously as a *muhibb al-watan*—"a lover of the homeland," or "a patriot." Here and in *Muhit al-Muhit* he called his pamphlets *wataniyyat.* As with the ascription for his pamphlets, al-Bustani adopted one of the *Nahda*'s key slogans—"Love of the homeland is an element of faith" *(hubb al-watan min al-iman)*—from Tahtawi's *wataniyyat,* perhaps because they were reproduced in *Hadiqat al-Akhbar* in the late 1850s.[16] Like al-Tahtawi, al-Bustani claimed that the aphorism had *hadith* status.[17] The Quranic term *al-iman* incorporates both the act and the content of faith.[18] For al-Bustani patriotism demanded a leap of faith, a commitment to loyalty even in adversity. Yet, he was mindful of any fatalism that this kind of faith might generate.

Perhaps quoting from *Surat al-Ra'd*, al-Bustani reminded his readers that "God will not change the state of a people unless they change themselves." In other words, mere faith in the homeland was not sufficient. What is required is something much more proactive: love.[19] *al-Hubb* is juxtaposed to all the ills of his society: selfishness, revengefulness, fanaticism, and idleness; but it also did work that no amount of international pity and charity could provide. Based on *al-iman,* love is "the magnet" that attracted diverse people to their homeland. Selfless, or unselfish, love must conquer the violent passions and rein in its ignorant perpetrators so that the homeland can guarantee ecumenical religiosity in this "Babel of religions, races, and confessions" that was "Syria."[20]

In *Nafir Suriyya,* al-Bustani recognized that "patriotism is an element of faith" was a concept liable to usurpation and abuse. But it was his nemesis, Ahmad Faris al-Shidyaq, who launched a blistering critique of "the false patriot." The false patriot would extol the virtues of the homeland, its natural beauty, its culture, and its history but would have nothing but contempt for his neighbors and compatriots, all the while reciting "to love one's homeland is part of faith." Shidyaq charged that there were very few patriots whose concern for the country was genuine. But when these few criticized their compatriots, they would do so as "kind educators and tender guardians." For them "life is not enjoyable if wealth is not shared by all." If "some people praise without being really concerned and some are concerned without praise," Shidyaq deemed "the latter are better."[21]

Shidyaq may have considered al-Bustani a "kind educator," given how *Nafir Suriyya* insisted that "the secret lies in the dweller—not the house."[22] The affective registers of loyalty that his pamphlets articulated did not just echo the official Tanzimat discourse emanating from Istanbul. They were significantly altered: whereas Ottoman and Egyptian reform discourse offered subjects *(ri'aya)* equality in return for loyalty to the state, al-Bustani's *hubb-al-watan,* "patriotism," most powerfully articulated in the fourth issue of *Nafir Suriyya,* promoted a contract of rights and duties between the inhabitants and their homeland. What mattered most was not the state but "the welfare of the homeland." The role of the state was important but external to the contract itself. This shift challenged the traditional legal concept of subject, *ra'iyya* (pl. *al-ri'aya*), and *Nafir Suriyya* issued the term only once.[23] Instead he often used the religiously inflected *'ibad* (subjects), *ahali* (commoners), or *bani* (folks) and their derivatives, which were popular in Bilad al-Sham but had no legal standing. Nor did he speak of or for *al-sha'ab*—the concept of "the people" emerged in Arabic political discourse only after 1862;[24] he also introduced the liberal concept of *al-insan*— the human being—which came to acquire legal status in international law and human rights discourse in the twentieth century.

The "compatriots" were divided into two types: the *'uqala',* the responsible thinkers, and the *awbash,* the hoodlums who "trade patriotism for fanaticism and sacrifice the well-being of the homeland for personal interests."[25] Although they did not "deserve to belong to the homeland," the whole reason for the anguished patriotism al-Bustani expressed in *Nafir Suriyya* was that, by hook or by crook, warts and all, all compatriots are in it together. As Bou Ali has put it, drawing on Lauren Berlant, "love as a political rhetoric meant [for al-Bustani] to empower the national subject while acknowledging the ill-fate of belonging to a nation."²⁶

The way love and faith sustained *al-watan* in *Nafir Suriyya* worked both on a biographical and on a societal level. For al-Bustani, the religious transgressor and cultural reformer, *al-watan* promised a secure space against violent passions and social apathy. Internal exile played a crucial role in al-Bustani's political imagination as he reclaimed personal as well as political sovereignty through the concept of *al-watan*. As a convert, he knew that identities were not fixed, and as a teacher with an evangelical disposition, he believed that people could overcome even their most basic instincts.

FIRST EXPRESSIONS OF ANTISECTARIANISM?

> There is a difference between someone who identifies prejudices and someone who identifies with a prejudice.
>
> —Salim al-Bustani, "al-Gharadh," *al-Jinan* (1870)

The most urgent task Butrus al-Bustani set himself with *Nafir Suriyya* was to name and shame the condition that stood in the way of patriotism and led to the violence. This task was all the more difficult because, for all his interest in the social— he coined the term *al-hay'a al-ijtima'iyya* here—the concept of sectarianism did not exist yet, neither as a principle of rule nor as one of social critique. *al-Ta'ifiyya*—the abstract noun for the Lebanese system of sectarian political representation—was introduced much later and institutionalized only in the French Mandate period.²⁷ In *Nafir Suriyya*, the noun *ta'ifa/tawa'if* contended with others and first appeared in al-Bustani's analysis only in relation to well-organized and productive animal collectives—ants, bees, and silkworms.[28] In the last three issues, *al-taʾifi/al-taʾifiyya* appear as adjectives among others—like personal *(shakhsi, nafsani, dhati)*, familial *(ʿaʾili)*, and confessional *(madhhabi)*—to specify the scourges of enmities *(ʿadawat)*, factionalisms *(tahazzubat)*, self-interests *(ghayat)*.

It was the noun *al-gharadh* (pl. *al-aghradh*) that appeared most frequently and most unexpectedly in those passages in which al-Bustani grappled with what we today call sectarianism.[29] We consider *gharadh/aghradh* to designate sectarianism as understood today, but in order to avoid overdetermination, we decided to translate the term in the context of how al-Bustani used it, as blind "prejudice" in favor of some predetermined group identity or, in some instances where political factionalism is explicitly invoked, as partisanship. If, as Kosellek has argued, history does not depend on language to happen, then sectarianism can exist *avant le mot*. al-Bustani explained the "fanaticism" and "factionalism" that led to the civil war as surface phenomena unleashed because Syrians "surrendered" to their "prejudices." But identifying *gharadh/aghradh* as the ultimate causation, his analysis remained limited to flaws in individual human behavior: unwillingness to reflect on the consequences of one's action, and the betrayal of traditions of neighborliness, as well as the epoch-defining spirit of altruism, public welfare, and civic responsibility. If secularism became the dominant panacea of sectarianism in the twentieth century, al-Bustani advocated a return to "true religion."[30]

The year 1860 continued to haunt the Beiruti *Nahda* long after al-Bustani stopped writing his pamphlets, and *al-gharadh* remained a conspicuous category of analysis to explain the violence in terms of "uncontrolled human instincts." In a lengthy article for *al-Jinan* his son Salim al-Bustani revisited *al-gharadh* with the passionate introspection that characterized many of his fictional writings. Although he returned to many of *Nafir Suriyya*'s themes, he was much less evangelical in his editorials than his father had been. It had been a decade since the civil war. The Ottomans had pacified Bilad al-Sham and economic and cultural life had resumed in Beirut, and he expressed frustration that partisanship and prejudices persisted. In fact, he realized that as soon as someone "defames" him with "spears of reproach" for his writings, he blames it on "ugly *prejudice* in his bile." He wondered if this response made him any better than those he criticized. How could he escape the temptation or charge of prejudice and partisanship if he and his father were so harsh in their judgment of their compatriots? Did patriotism not engender new forms of harmful passions? Having set up the problem as a bodily condition—located in the bile—the article justified their social criticism. Being partial to the common good is noble but "the hero of the age is patient in all situations." Still, prejudice against the "conscripts" of partisanship was legitimate. "The quality of rational persons depends on their ability to consider time and place" both in praise and in condemnation. "Prejudice" may have many sources: "profit, kinship, love, loss, hatred, envy, proclivity for revenge, religion, conditions of race, and distress." Some are good and necessary. For example, "if one tribe attacks another, the defending tribe must adhere to *gharadh* in order to defend oneself in a unified way." In such instances *gharadh* is best rendered as "personal interest." But generally, Salim al-Bustani insists, *gharadh* should not be tolerated. Thus, "factional mobilization for one tribe against another, or devotion to a religion based on exclusive belonging and enmity of other religions, jeopardizes truth and justice."[31]

The Bustanis' line of argument may strike the reader as somewhat naïve. It certainly does not provide answers to current problems of sectarianism. But, as Ussama Makdisi has argued, antisectarian dispositions emerged in their writings starting with *Nafir Suriyya,* even though there was—again—no name for it yet.[32] If sectarianism and antisectarianism existed in nineteenth-century Bilad al-Sham before anyone had a word for it, then this has repercussions for the relationship between history and language in the *Nahda* and beyond. To be sure, semantics alone do not constitute discourse, but discourse analysis without historicizing language use also impedes the meaningful translation of historical texts such as *Nafir Suriyya.* And it is to the translation of this text that the second part of this book now turns.

PART II

Translation of *The Clarion*
of Syria

CHAPTER 6

Clarion 1

Beirut, September 29, 1860[1]

Countrymen,

News of the spell of atrocities and abominations committed this summer by the troublemakers in our midst has reached the corners of the Earth. All over the civilized world, it has drawn pity and gloom, on one hand, and anger and wrath, on the other. Yet, we witness charity pour in from all sides to help the needy. Armies from every land are also heading our way to protect the weak and to punish the guilty and the aggressor.

All too often we have noticed how the victorious faction boasts about its deeds, declaring "we have satisfied our honor" and the like.[2] What the victors do not seem to realize is that the civilized world has nothing but disgust, contempt, and rage for what they take pride in. It regards their deeds as the work of savage barbarians devoid of humanity, character, chivalry, and faith, the work of thieves and bandits. That is why the civilized world has now joined forces to unleash the worst of punishment on the oppressors and to teach them a lesson. At the same time, we see the majority of the vanquished fall under the illusion that the armies came only to help them seek revenge and sanction the looting and bloodletting of their adversaries. This is nothing but a distortion of the true intentions of the Great Powers. If this wronged faction plans to act with this interpretation in mind, they would expose themselves to rage and would deserve harsher punishment than the victors. Sympathy for them would turn into harsh treatment, and as a result they would be subject to great harm.

Let the victors know that the time for their bravery and prowess has passed, and that their brandishing of arms has become impermissible and unacceptable. The only way forward then is to trust in their government and the friendly powers that are disembarking here to restore peacefulness and security in their quarters. They need to wait patiently for the philanthropic efforts that these states have agreed upon, for these efforts will duly take into account the opinions of the people and require their assistance.

It is a blatant mistake for the victorious faction to run away and leave their hometowns under the illusion that they can escape the punishment they deserve. Running away can only lead to the breakup of families and the ruin of the country. Moreover, it causes undue suspicion toward the innocent among the runaways. Neither the victorious party nor anyone else should assume that these states sent their representatives to take the side of one group over another, or to protect a certain group or avenge another just because they are Christian or non-Christian. As far as we know, they came only to protect the rights of man and to enforce the principles of justice and rule of law. No innocent group needs to be afraid, and we have no evidence that collective accusations will be levied on any one faction.

And so, countrymen, the destruction and damage that afflicted our land are unparalleled in historical chronicles. Most of you are well aware of the reasons behind this destruction.

This pains all the more the heart of every eyewitness and patriot. Even if this destruction appears to affect only some of you, it is, in fact, a matter affecting all. Any loss incurred comes out of the national treasury, and the loss of every soul is the loss of society as a whole.

Countrymen,

You drink the same water, you breathe the same air. The language you speak is the same, and so are the ground you tread, your welfare, and your customs. You may still be intoxicated from drinking your compatriots' blood, or disoriented by the calamities you have suffered. But very soon you must wake up from this stupor and realize the meaning of my advice and where your welfare lies. This is what I intend to convey to you here. I hope that I can continue writing to you, and I ask God to guide you toward knowing your own good and the good of your country. May your hearts embrace the teachings and principles of the faith you believe in. And may God preserve you.

From a patriot

CHAPTER 7

Clarion 2

October 8, 1860[1]

Countrymen,

When news of the unrest and transgressions that befell this country reached Sultan ʿAbd al-Majid, he was deeply moved. This is evident to anybody who reads the decree issued in early July 1860 to his excellency, the great statesman Fuʾad Pasha, who was sent by the High Porte as an emissary to these lands. Imperial measures to avert inequity, stop the continued disturbances, and achieve peace and security are further proof of his highness's concern for the seriousness of the problem, his care for his subjects' welfare, and his compassion for them.

Moreover, the written and spoken statements that General Fuʾad Pasha expressed in this Sublime Decree upon his auspicious arrival on the shores of this country have promised peace, security, and justice to all subjects, and have raised everybody's expectations that his highness will fulfill those benevolent intentions and righteous promises.[2]

Countrymen,

You must be running out of patience because you have spent so much time humiliated and away from your abodes. You have grown homesick and want to return to your birthplace; or, as they say, the country misses its people. Many of you have since lost your dearest friends and children and many of you are sick, barefoot, and needy. Your whole condition elicits sadness and grief. The lack of adequate retribution for the wrongdoing that you have suffered and the lack of compensation for the damages that you have incurred have undoubtedly worsened your plight and anxiety. As you know, to build is more difficult than to destroy, especially when the destruction is committed by the troublemakers of a vast country and in such a short period of time. Can a single engineer, no matter how competent, restore its former state of beauty as quickly as it has been destroyed—especially if he is a perfectionist? This is what the current state of affairs has come to.

Countrymen,

We lament your condition. We are aware of your distress and your loss. They add to our pain and sadness and force us to excuse your obstinance and your complaints. However, we consider that the best approach to set things straight is not to rush things, but to deliberate carefully and to avoid measures that would only worsen the devastation. The only way going forward is to place your confidence and trust in those in charge and to give yourselves reason to hope that they will exert their efforts in supporting the oppressed and carrying out the justice that is due to them. The fact that the greatest powers of the world are lending you their attention in the desire to alleviate your hardship, grant you your peace, and help you obtain your rights should fill you with trust, confidence, and patience.

Countrymen,

Many of you say, "Whoever is patient succeeds and whoever is obstinate sins," and "Patience is the key to relief," and

"Obstinance is followed by regret," and "It is prudent not to rush things so as not to spoil them." Yes, blindness of the heart befell the Israelites because of their impatience.[3] Rather than follow their example, would it not be better for your own sake to take their fate as a warning and a moral tale? How we long for your prompt return to your abodes so you may live in security, comfort, and luxury. Your way out of this is to be thankful and patient and ask God to bless those who saved you by preventing the spread of destruction, sedition, the meddling of the wicked, and the bloodletting. Pray to God that those in whose hands the affairs of the people are entrusted will guide you onto the righteous path. May He support them in their initiatives to do good deeds and protect the rights of man.

Countrymen,

It may occasionally cross your mind that this country was punished by God. It's true. Do not think otherwise, but welcome this idea with an open heart so that it may remind you that to Him you shall return. For then He shall hold back from inflicting harm. Otherwise, His hand may weigh down heavily because God will not change the state of a people unless they change themselves.[4]

Our hope is that you read through this and the previous pamphlets with a spirit of love, goodwill, and simplicity. Both were written with good intentions and without prejudice by someone who shares your feelings and is pained by your calamities, which are also his. May God preserve you.

From a patriot

CHAPTER 8

Clarion 3

October 15, 1860

Countrymen,

What has become of your country that it is dressed in mourning? Why are your mountains and hilltops desolate and your valleys and plains looking so forlorn? Why is there tension in your towns and villages? Why are your strongmen broken, your women wailing, your virgins crying, and your widows and orphans in such a sorry state of deep humiliation and wretchedness? Why is Damascus, the jewel in the crown of Syria and one of the greatest and most famous of ancient cities, set amid forests and ponds under willow trees lining the Barada River, now draped in black, weeping for its young men and women, and mourning the loss of its wealth, riches, markets, and resources.

What has befallen you now? You hear voices wailing over a lost loved one, or a fugitive friend, or an imprisoned husband, or an only son in captivity, or an abducted daughter. Hither you hear sighs from inconsolable hearts overcome with sorrow and grief, broken hearts that have been filled with chalices of despair and depression. And thither is a deep, uninterrupted moan from a heart whose troubles are mixed with incurable maladies and unbearable pains.

What has befallen us, now that we see over there a man hiding in a cave, and another who has taken shelter in the thick woods among wild animals, and yet another who, like the brother-slayer Cain, is a fugitive who has lost his way with no one calling him in?

What has befallen us now that we see in this city of Beirut multitudes of privileged and common people alike, queuing up to ask for charity, when most used to be alms givers themselves?

These scenes are undoubtedly terrifying and saddening. How could this happen? Who are those who appeased the devil and inflicted this much natural and moral destruction? The answer to all of this can be culled from what we have written previously. Time does not permit further elaboration. Nor is it of any use to look back at the recent past. Rather we must turn our attention to the future in order to alleviate impending calamities and to stop their negative effects and wicked consequences.

Countrymen,

Summer, the season of comfort and few needs, has elapsed. It was a season in which many of you may have been satisfied with just the foot of a mountain for a bed, a tree or the sky's dome for a cover, and the stars as guardians. Now the trees that have offered you shade are starting to shed their leaves in preparation for another season. I sense menacing clouds rising from the west to do battle with the current climate, to block off those guardian stars, and to alert us to the looming winter—the season of meager means and many needs—which is charging toward us with its storms, snow, and bitter cold.

Countrymen,

Ant colonies have finished stocking up for winter and have dug holes in the ground to protect themselves from winter's harshness. Swarms of bees have brought in their harvests and built sturdy honeycombs stacked with their precious supply to settle in a hive of comfort and protection. By contrast, many of our brothers, sons of Adam, and our compatriots barely have enough means to sustain them for the day, and—even worse— have no houses for shelter, no clothes to protect them from the severe cold, no furniture to accommodate them, and no storage for provisions. This is what makes caring for their future so very vital, yet so precarious.

Countrymen,

Westerners say, "Time is gold," but for our poor brothers "time is life," because every passing day costs the homeland the life of many of its sons. Therefore, as we pointed out before, it is the duty of the oppressed to be patient, as it is the religious, moral, and civic duty of the treacherous oppressors and those who are in positions of responsibility to use effective means to achieve the necessary security immediately and, if possible, to offer food, shelter, clothes, and other outstanding needs to the oppressed. It is also the duty of those with pride, conscience, and pity, whoever they might be, to exert their efforts and dedicate their energy toward helping the oppressed rather than sacrificing them at the altar of personal pleasures, gains, interests, or whatever they may be.

Countrymen,

It seems that security was hatched only recently through the hard labor of those in charge of this country. Now it lies swaddled—as per Eastern custom—in the cradle, susceptible to numerous and varying afflictions. Were it to be surrounded by strong guards and the most capable and wise physicians from East and West, with all their surgical tools and all sorts of medicinal drugs, we trust that this nascent security would be shielded from the vagaries of time. We also hope that their expertise would provide effective means for the country to grow quickly and reach the age of maturity in a reasonable amount of time.

Countrymen,

We like to draw your attention to the fact that it is preferable to live by the labor of your hands and the sweat on your forehead than to knock on doors and rely on charity, whose wells are neither inexhaustible nor ever lasting. We also warn you against the harm that unemployment does to your body, mind, and soul. And especially to the stricken among you, we say: rely on God, caretaker of the orphaned and the widowed who does not ignore the sighs of the wretched poor.

Countrymen,

This has been a lengthy address, but we will not conclude without saying the following: True religion will promote virtue and prevent vice. And every religion that does not have this characteristic does not deserve to be called religion. One of the virtues of Christianity, compared to other religions, is that it asks to love even one's enemies. It is undoubtedly one of the most difficult commands to fulfill. However, this difficulty does not exempt Christians in general from striving for it at all times, in all places, and in all situations. While Christianity commands its followers to turn their right cheek to those who hit them on the left and to meet evil with good, it does not forbid its adherents from demanding their rights. Rather it permits them to defend themselves and seek their rights, but not through the spirit of revenge or the love of reprisal. For there is nothing Christian about insisting on hate and spitefulness and maintaining the spirit of revenge and reprisal. In closing, I ask God to guide you toward understanding this truism and to give you the strength to follow through this path. May He preserve you.

From a patriot

CHAPTER 9

Clarion 4

October 25, 1860

Countrymen,

We have talked about the homeland at length in our pamphlets. We did so because the homeland is the dearest thing to those who love it, and it is the most pleasantly coined word adorning the Arabic language. Syria, which is known as Barr al-Sham and Arabistan, is our homeland with all its diverse plains, coastlines, mountains, and barren lands. The inhabitants of Syria, regardless of their religious beliefs, their physical features, their ethnicities, and their general diversity, are all our compatriots. For the homeland resembles a chain of many rings. One end of the chain represents our place of residence, birthplace, or ancestral home. At the other end lies our country and everyone in it. The center and magnet of these two poles are our heart. The homeland holds strong sway over its children. It draws and holds them within its embrace, however loose this embrace might be. It also captures their hearts and pulls them closer to their homeland so that they may return even when their lives are more comfortable abroad.

"If homelands were not to die for, the ill-fated homelands would turn into ruin." The more we identify with the homeland's material and moral aspects, the more we are attracted to it, and the fonder we become of it.[1] For we deem our house to be the best of houses, our compatriots the best of people. As the saying rightly goes: "Seek the host—not the house." For whoever travels the world sees as clearly as daylight that no matter how meritorious a homeland is, the evils of its people can ruin it. Conversely, no matter how rotten it is in and of itself, the merits of its people compensate for it.

Countrymen,

People of the homeland have rights vis-à-vis their country which in turn has obligations toward them. It goes without saying that the more these rights are fulfilled, the more people grow attached to their country, and the more desirous and pleased they are in rendering those duties. Among the obligations that a country owes its people is to secure their precious right to life, honor, and prosperity.[2] These obligations also include upholding civil, moral, and religious freedoms, especially the freedom of conscience in confessional matters. Many were the countries that were sacrificed for this freedom.

Compatriots love their country more whenever they sense that it is theirs. Their happiness lies in its civilizational development and comfort while their misery lies in its destruction and misfortune. Their ability to take part in its affairs and to get involved in its welfare increases their desire for its success and their enthusiasm for its progress. The more responsibility is placed on them, the more intense and resolute these feelings become. Therefore, one of the most important duties of our compatriots is to love their homeland.

It has been mentioned in a *hadith:* "Love of the homeland is an element of faith."[3] Many were the people who sacrificed their lives and all that they own out of love for their country. As for those who exchange patriotism for confessional fanaticism and who sacrifice the welfare of the homeland for personal interests, they do not deserve to belong to the homeland. They are its enemies. Those who do not expend any effort to prevent or alleviate incidences harmful to the country are equally its enemies. In these difficult times, few compatriots have displayed their patriotism. The ugly deeds of those who fired the first shot and those who lifted the first stone off the mouth of the dreadful volcano that is torching the country and its people have forever left a black mark in the annals of Syria. Likewise, those who did not work hard to muzzle the barrel of that gun and the mouth of that volcano are guilty; they have fallen short in their duties toward their homeland.

Let us take this opportunity to make clear the feelings of gratitude and welcome toward our brothers who are on the other side of the Atlantic and toward their children who are guests in our country. They have shown and are still showing continuous assistance to our compatriots. Their generosity shames us.

Countrymen,

Our country is world renowned for its water, air, and soil. It is the most proud and praiseworthy. Yet for a number of generations, it has been afflicted by the corruption of uncivilized segments of its people. That is why you see it increasingly lagging behind other countries and becoming even more backward following the recent unrest. But we hope that with the help of God, with the stamina of our Sublime State and the friendly Great Powers, this current setback, whose echoes have reached the corners of the inhabited Earth, will turn into the beginning of great goodness and usher in a new age for Syria. The following may suffice as a reminder for those who are weary:

> Tell those who carry a burden: burdens do not last
> Happiness dies out; worries become a thing of the past

Countrymen,

We warn you of obstinacy, despotism, fanaticism, and idleness. They are devoid of goodness. And we alert you to these precious words: "Do unto others as you would have them do unto you." We remind you of this as well: Man's true homeland is not in this world but in the spiritual world beyond the grave. There he shall remain till the horn is sounded and he is resurrected for Judgment. Alas, many of our brethren have gone this year to this other, everlasting homeland. Numerous are the causes but death is one. It is therefore incumbent that we prepare for that homeland and the Day of Judgement.

From a patriot

CHAPTER 10

Clarion 5

November 1, 1860

Countrymen,

The worst thing under the firmament is war, and the most horrendous among them are civil wars, which break out between the commoners of a single country and which are often triggered by trivial causes and for ignoble aims. Civil wars are not only the negation of justice and a transgression against the rights of those in command. They show no respect for the most generous feelings and most noble rights of man. These include national fraternity, harmony, gratitude, and kindness toward neighbours and those compatriots who possess chivalry and humanity. The war that erupted this year was one of the most horrendous civil wars. Its flames have wrought enormous damage onto our religious, moral, and civil interests and public welfare. As a result, the country and the world have lost so much and at great costs and risks.

Countrymen,

How can we excuse the sons of our homeland in the eyes of foreigners? How else but to point to their stupidity, their lack of civility, and the triumph of their carnal appetites over their rational faculties? Perhaps the magnanimous will excuse them, given the extraordinary circumstances they acted under. For what does one expect from a land whose inhabitants are bands of many tribes divided by character traits, moods, prejudice, and self-interest, a land where few care about public welfare and many do not feel this country is theirs.[1]

Syria lies between two countries, Egypt and the Ottoman empire, which have often pulled it in different directions. Within a single generation, it has tilted at times to one side and at other times to the other.[2] In both instances, Syria has unfortunately found itself in the peripheries of each empire. It was far removed from the center of government, that is to say, from the capital of both empires. Its tutelage was thus left to the mercy of the same people who were responsible for Syria's demise, as history and our forefathers have taught us.

Syria is also the birthplace and stage of many conflicting civil and religious prejudices whose organization and origins are at odds with each other. We know of no other country whose fate has endured such tribulations as Syria and yet remained inhabited and home to a people that, despite all, have kept their morals, honor, chivalry, and enthusiasm. These characteristics give us hope for Syria's advancement and civilization, as long as the people who uphold them are supported by a modern system of governance that works both for the welfare of the country and for the comfort of its subjects. Is it possible then for someone who considers what we said without bias and prejudice not to excuse these people, given what he sees of mutual schisms, estrangement, and shortcomings? Is it possible not to protest against all the delusions and difficulties he sees in their politics and the way they run things?

Countrymen,

When we inspect this land's historical record to search for lessons of what the future might hold, we regret to say that this history is full of wars and catastrophes. We also find that your prejudice has, like an ugly black spot, shamelessly replaced patriotism at the center of each page of our history. Even in the best of times, when the land was basking in ease, prosperity, fertility, and peace, this wicked carnal principle has often raised its head and frothed wildly. Inherited from barbarians, prejudice left behind destruction and peril and squandered the land's wealth and its families.

During the days of Cairo's rule over Syria, a group of patriots assembled to contain this form of partisanship and tried to weaken or destroy it.[3] But shortly afterward, the shrewd workings of time and the events of those days let partisanship escape again. As it rose up with great might, its wicked effects began to take hold. It is too bad they did not put a millstone around its neck and throw it into the bottomless depths of the sea!

This wicked concept takes different colors at every stage. It once took the form of notable rivalries such as the one between the Qaysi and Yamani factions, and then between the Jumblats and the Yazbakis.[4] One of its ugliest forms has appeared in these last few years. It took on names sacred to its people—names like Christian and Druze, and then Muslim and Christian. These sacred names had long been buried under the previous ones of the Qaysi/Yamani and Jumblat/Yazbak splits, but the concept has appropriated these sacred and old names, realizing the magical and formidable force that they hold when used in the context of what the people of our country call "the source of attachment"—that is, kinship.[5] As such, this wicked concept served the machinations of the most powerful leaders of prejudices with the result that its power multiplied and its effects became far-reaching.

On a pitch-dark night, we observed from this city a series of terrifying blazes ascending from the Matn. It was as if we saw the fire of partisanship go up along with the burning houses.[6] Should partisanship die out as we had envisioned, you shall rejoice in prosperity, comfort, and security. We send you our condolences and ask that you do not regret its demise despite the frequently invoked saying "He who has no partisanship has no religion." For such a saying has been passed down generations from barbaric peoples whose religion is founded on prejudice. But what is the benefit of a religion if it is based on prejudice?

Countrymen,

We have often heard you say that this was the third bout of ruinous events in the span of less than twenty years. Now that you have tried civil wars time and again and have weighed its gains and losses, we ask you: What have you won? Have any of you become a king, a marshal, or a minister? Have you attained a higher rank and status, or increased your wealth or fame? What have you achieved other than the bereavement of widows and orphaned children, moral depravation, poverty, and destruction—in both this life and the hereafter—as well as humiliation and belittlement in the eyes of wise men and foreigners? What has come about other than decimating the number of able hands upon whose hard work the reconstruction of the country and the comfort of its people depend? What has come about other than depriving the country of its richest, wisest, smartest, and most able men?

Now, is it not better for your own sake to replace blind prejudices—which is merely a euphemism for excessive self-love—with patriotism, affection, concord, and unity, all of which are prerequisites for the country's success? Is it not in your interest to shun the cursed devil, extend the carpet of hospitality, remember the harmony of olden times, and roll up your sleeves for the sake of alleviating these catastrophes and making up for this destruction? Are you not aware that you are your brother's keeper, not his enemy? Should not this be the voice of the wise among you and the opinion of those who have your best interest at heart and do not wish to leave your affairs to chance? If so, then the guilty among you should gladly and voluntarily pay their dues. And those who have been victims of injustice should pursue their rights kindly and patiently under the aegis of those in charge, for their authority is bestowed by God, and they did not carry the sword in vain. Countrymen, this is for your own benefit.

Countrymen,

It had occurred to us frequently—before the recent events—to sound this clarion in order to alert you to the vicious effects of civil wars. But having observed the condition of the people and that they were bent on playing out the scenario in their head, we and other wise people figured that the sweet sound of the patriot's clarion would have been drowned out by the crude drumbeat of prejudices and ill intent. So we held our breath.

Now that we have seen with our own eyes the burning fire of partisanship, we decided to speak out where regrettably we have been silent before. We consider this belated call a modest service to our homeland in the hope that it will be well received despite its shortcomings. Our duty is to write and to remind you. Your duty is to read and reflect. And what ultimately comes to pass is in the hands of God, the facilitator. May He preserve you.

From a patriot

CHAPTER II

Clarion 6

November 8, 1860

Losses and Gains of the Homeland

Countrymen,

The homeland's losses and damages due to the recent unrest have been so costly that it is difficult to imagine their extent.[1] The precise calculation of such losses requires the skills of a talented accountant. They are divided into material losses, which is our focus now, and moral ones, which—God willing—we will elaborate on later. Material losses include the country's houses, seasonal staples, revenues, harvests, belongings, cattle and the like that have been damaged by fire, destruction, vandalism, and theft. Losses also include what has been siphoned out of the country through bribery, treachery, and extortion, or by other means. As for what remains in the hands of local usurpers, they do not count as losses since they simply changed hands within our homeland.

If we add the value of the approximately thirty thousand burnt-down houses to the value of the buildings and harvests that have been destroyed all over the country, the total will amount to 367 million piasters (around 367 million francs), which comes close to three and a half times the value of Syria's annual revenue of silk (estimated at two thousand qantars per year). This is an approximate balance sheet put together from reliable sources. We would rather not go over it in any detail lest we leave the door open to arguments and objections. The actual value of the damages is likely to be even higher than our estimates because, except in rare cases, the value of possessions in the eyes of their owners is always higher than the real value or the one decided by an impartial outsider. Moreover, some people who fear that their claims will be devalued or slightly reduced may exaggerate their estimated losses so that final compensation is at least close to what they honestly thought they deserved. This means that those who provide honest estimates clearly risk incurring losses.

If only everyone were to agree to present accurate estimates, even if they incur a loss! For loss—no matter how great it is—is preferable, more acceptable, and more honorable when borne with honesty than any dishonorable gain regardless how exorbitant it is. If only there was among us a rational and intelligent person who can propose a solution to this problem while balancing between conscience and coffer. Whatever solution he may present will not work unless there is mutual trust between the people and the government, and unless the perpetrators pay for these extensive damages according to the law, customs, religion, and the political process.

Countrymen,

No matter how vast and devastating the aforementioned losses were, eventually the might of kings or the hard work of ordinary people can, with God's blessing, compensate all or some of them. But there are losses, not even a tiny fraction of which all the kings of the Earth together could compensate, even if they mustered all their men and money, expertise and will power. For who could return a father to an orphan, a husband to a widow, an only son to an impotent elder, or a dear daughter to a bereaved old woman? God alone is the father of the orphan, lord of the widow, the aid of the impotent, the crutch of the despairing. He alone has the power to cool the passions of the heart of these poor ones, give solace, mend the broken hearts, and balm their incurable, open wounds.

You realize that losses of this kind are not minor. It is estimated that twenty thousand people died in the unrest. These include those who were ravaged by the blade of the sword, and those who were killed by accident or in revenge, and those who died from fear and anxiety, and from dreadful living conditions and sheer fatigue. They also include martyred children who were sacrificed at the altar of savage barbarity. We had seen in them the next generation who should surpass us with their civility, knowledge, and culture. At every sunset the numbers of the dead increase and at every sunrise many more are transferred from the books of the living to the registers of the dead. If we were to pay reparations for them, they would reach at least six hundred million piasters. But it is far from us to attach a price to the creatures of God who are more precious than the entire material world.

If only the destruction and losses of this catastrophe would end so that we stop counting more numbers. The prospects for the future are obscure. Yes, very bleak and unknown to us. How much we wish that new paths be opened for us so that we can plead for better turns! So far we do not know when the time will come for the sun of hope and comfort to rise over Syria and never to set again. We ask God to look with kindness and mercy on this ill-fated country.

Countrymen,

One of the material losses was that so much of the land lay fallow this year because of the lack of cattle and seeds. This has multiplied the tribulations and pushed many of the people into beggary. But who guarantees us that the gates of charity will remain open and will not be blocked by an iron bolt and brass lock before the end of the impending winter? What is the state of this impoverished multitude that has been thrown onto the shoulders of the giving by the ordeals of the age?

Fifty thousand active men have been rendered unemployed. Work has now been suspended for six months, and we do not know when this state of affairs will end. Shops are closed, livelihood and manufacture suspended. What pen can calculate such losses? The Syria we knew six months ago, with its distinguished character among the Ottoman empire's lands, its opulence, comfort, and wonderful progress in the field of architecture, has fallen. In a way it was different from the rest of the empire. Yes, it has fallen indeed! And it is unlikely to recover from this devastating demise for many years to come, save by miracle or some extraordinary feat.

Whoever inspects the financial books of the imperial powers will notice that vast funds have been allocated to solving the Syrian Question, and will see that the account has not been closed yet. New accounts of material losses inflicted on Syria continue to be registered. It is thus fair to judge that all that it possesses is not enough to settle the account even if it sold itself, unless it is agreed that the debt be paid by what the Ottoman Treasury owes Syria. Only then may Syria rise above this crippling debt while remaining, as long as it exists, morally beholden to the countries that aided it.

The tally of debts owed to foreign states based on the losses to foreign residents due to looting of their properties, damages,

waste of time, closure of their shops, and so on is enormous.
Obviously, Syria cannot even hope to pay back all these foreign
claims from its own treasury.

Countrymen,

We should not conclude this discussion without mentioning
some of Syria's elusive gains. One of them is national charity.
Since this remained within the country, it counts toward both
liabilities and assets and as such does not feature in the accounting books. Although these donations hold enormous value, most
of them were allotted in silence. Taken each separately, they are
barely discernable, even through a magnifying glass. Most ordinary people who made donations to alleviate this calamity have
given more than they can afford while many of the wealthy have
yet to participate in this blessed act of charity. The latter collect
money and do not know for whom they collect; what they have
kept from the mouths of the needy despite all their wealth they
will end up paying all at once to those who may not even return
the favor with merciful prayers.

As for state aid, it amounts to around fifty thousand purses.[2]
If these purses are to be considered a loan, charity, or goodwill
gesture on behalf of the perpetrators, then, for obvious reasons,
we need to list them under both liabilities and assets in the
country's accounts. In all civilized countries, the wealth and
poverty of the government treasury are equated with the wealth
of its subjects and vice versa. As for American and European
charitable donations, they, too, are estimated at around fifty
thousand purses. We have to offer unconditional gratitude
because without them many would have died out of hunger and
miserable living conditions. Since the value of such generosity is
always double that of the donation, what is owed must be listed
as twice what was donated. Our hope is that the people of our

country do not turn away from the noble motto "Blessed are those who give more than they take." May they strive to be the spring of largesse as they have been its recipients.

Some are under the illusion, or wish to pretend they are, that these charitable acts are due to the magnanimity of kings or the generosity of states. In fact, they are the sacrifices and offerings of subjects as ordinary as those receiving them. They are the fruits of the hard work of widows and orphans. They come from the altruism of small children and the sweat on the foreheads of workers and professionals. The heart of aid recipients who care to examine this truth will surely bleed when they make use of the assistance. One expects them not to take lightly donations borne out of morsels of food earned with pain and money earned through hard, tiresome work.

Given this reality, a clear conscience is required that monitors the distribution and acceptance of these charities in order to make sure that they are received with gratitude and honesty. As for the claim that the Syrian unrest is the start of a worldwide war causing total destruction, we believe it is baseless. Our limited insight tells us that the desired goal of bringing peace and prosperity back to Syria can be achieved through extensive means. Otherwise, we are left to conclude that the world has gone old and mad or to agree with some of the astrologers who, guided by their visions and observations, have ordained that the Day of Judgment has arrived at our gates. If this were really the case, we would not need to feel sorry that it is too late or too early; we would need to worry about neither past nor future losses and destructions.

Countrymen,

This unrest has certainly affected your feelings deeply. But if it has turned your hearts into stone, encouraged you to sin and be disobedient or to ignore religious, moral, and civic duties, then rest assured that the aforementioned losses were grossly underestimated. God's hand will strike harder and spiritual devastation will be added to the temporal one.

If this unrest led you to repent to God, steer away from sins, hatred, and enmities, mend your errant ways, and uphold religious scriptures and principles, then we overestimated our loss. In that case, the homeland would gain tremendously. Though caused by the evil of sin and corruption of the hearts, this blow could, in fact, become an epiphany for you, your children, and your country to seek self-improvement. As the Lord said: "if you obey me and keep to my commandments, you will reap the fruits of the Earth, and if you don't obey me you will be struck down by the blade of the sword."

Countrymen,

Heed what hath been said. Do not say that now is not the time to be religious, that it is all falling on deaf ears, that it is like flogging a dead horse. These and other clichés like them are just obsessions perpetuated by the enemies of our common good who roar like lions ready to devour us. Those who are forewarned must listen and those who are the spiritual guides must pay attention; the well-being of the soul ought not be sacrificed on the altar of the comfort of the body. For this is the right time, and this is the time for salvation.

Awake! Awake! Oh Shepherds of Israel and leaders of the people, why are you asleep and feigning ignorance? Behold the ferocious lions who come to devour flock and shepherd alike.[3]

From a patriot

CHAPTER 12

Clarion 7

November 19, 1860[1]

Moral Losses of the Homeland

Countrymen,

The moral losses that befell the homeland as a result of the recent unrest are many and varied. They are even more criminal and evil than the material losses mentioned in the previous address. Among the moral losses is the loss of the concord that our fathers and grandfathers bequeathed us. This loss is tremendous in itself but, as the astute critic knows, the national concord was already shaky before the eruption of the recent civil war. Indeed, the current losses of the homeland only increased the estrangement and antagonism between different communities and among members of the same community.[2]

Those who observed carefully the country's state of affairs before the current crisis and noticed how the hearts were filled with malice and hatred predicted that these thick dark clouds were going to result in muddied and sullied living conditions. They also expected that the filth of hatred and extreme prejudice that was stored up in people's chests for many years would at some point in time erupt in a violent outburst. The slightest trigger would lead to the destruction of everything and everyone in its wake because the deep wound inflicted by the treachery of earlier wars and unrests was sealed before it was cleansed from pernicious infections.

Hearts suppressed their hatred and anger while waiting for an opportune moment to shoot their sharp arrows at those standing in the way of these hearts' ascendant power and prestige. These wicked wars have in turn placed a father's killer in front of his son, turned the killer of a son into his father's neighbor, placed a thief of a robbed mother in front of her daughter, and positioned the defamer of a daughter next to her mother. Zayd's cap was placed on ʿUbayd's head and Hind's necklace on Daʿad's neck.³ Memories of such injustices came to be stirred, at opportune moments, in order to arouse the malicious feelings that were—under the effect of songs and lullabies—dormant but not asleep. What is expected from a people and from neighbors in such miserable states when they have no religious, moral, or civil wisdom to restrain them? Rather, enmity, social divisions, and family factions were constantly mobilized for purposes we are neither too blind to see nor too foolish to see through.

Countrymen,

It is no secret how dangerous it is for a country or district to fail to punish murderers or to grant free rein to people who have become used to looting and shedding blood. Such men who have inherited these traits from their fathers and forefathers by nature and nurture have often experienced the pleasures of impunity—even rewards—associated with their deeds.

Is it possible for a country and a people that are in such a wretched state as we are to sustain peace, concord, and calm for any length of time? The reality of the current situation proves that the honest answer is clearly "no"—that it seems absolutely impossible. If we remain silent, the rocks of Syria will speak out loud, as will the blood of its people. We should not resign ourselves to the claims that the peoples' feelings are noble and strong enough to weather the sword and the bullets. For while those who are free from such violent aspirations exhibit some of the most pleasant and delicate traits, we see that the people with prejudice are still active and mobilized.

We hope that, this time around, matters do not fall under the old rule of "let bygones be bygones." This was about to happen again were it not for the arrival of the great statesman, His Excellency Fuʾad Pasha. May the remedies be stronger and may the sanctions be more effective this time. Despite the constant delays we are witnessing, this hope is not without grounds. As the poet's saying goes:

> A people stand to lose from vacillation
> When decisiveness would have solved the situation

Countrymen,

The homeland needs concord for its survival, construction, and prosperity. We know from experience that the loss of concord is one of the most painful and pernicious losses. But someone may wonder: "Is the return to concord possible after what happened?" For as the poet says:

> Hearts are like bottles of glass
> When broken cannot be recast

It is clear that this verse contains as much exaggeration as wisdom. Perhaps it was uttered by a pre-Islamic poet who did not live long enough to see it refuted by history or, occasionally,

by general experience. For concord, unlike discord, is a natural
instinct of mankind that denotes companionship—as opposed
to estrangement—and not forgetfulness, as some claim.
Concord was indispensable for the rise of mankind and the
promotion of the interests and well-being of human existence.
This is why our hopes for a return to concord are high, in the
long run at least. And we thought it befitting to alter the previous verse to read:

> Glass bottles are broken forever
> But estranged hearts can be mended together

One should not understand our words to mean that we advocate
a return to concord with blood shedders. No one who values the
good of the public and the country over the good of the individual or groups of individuals would call for such a thing. And it is
no secret that the return of concord and its very existence, persistence, and growth depend on certain conditions, most
urgently on the following.

First: We need living and attentive religions to teach their
children to view those who hold different beliefs neither with
contempt nor with scorn, as is now often the case, but with care
and affection, as among members of one family whose father is
the homeland, its mother the Earth, and God the single creator,
with all members created out of the same substance, sharing the
same destiny. God does not favor one individual over another for
their title or group association, but for their knowledge, piety,
reason, virtue, neighborliness, and upholding of the rights of
mankind and the common good. Human beings are valued by
two attributes: what they feel and what they say. For us, laws are
to be obeyed, the rights they bestow upheld, and the duties they
entail fulfilled. Anyone who studies the histories of religious

communities and peoples knows the harm visited upon religion and people when religious and civil matters, despite the vast difference between them, are mixed. This mixing should not be allowed on religious or political grounds. But how often has it had a hand in the present destruction? God knows, and so do you. And since this patriot is not from the band of fools, he also knows.

Second: We need wakeful and firm local authorities capable of drawing the line against transgressors without exposing their inability to draw on support from outside their area of jurisdiction. They will treat all classes equally and provide law-abiding people with full religious, moral, and civil rights. These rights are not privileges dependent on affiliation to a person or to a group of people, but they are rights as such.

Third: We need agreed-upon legislation, just provisions and legal prosecution based on evidence rather than personal favoritism. These need to be in harmony with the times and independent from religious laws.

Fourth: We need to reject blind partisanship so that a family or a group cannot be condemned because of the actions of one of its members. Likewise, the homeland as a whole cannot be condemned because of the guilt of some of its sons; nor can we neglect the many charitable deeds of its helpful and humane sons. To maintain concord effectively we advise you to avoid this natural inclination to condemn an entire race and to attack it because of the failings of some of its members. In fact, it appears that, more than in other successful countries, the welfare and construction in this country, where divisions are so rife, depend heavily on these concerns; and their absence is one of the most important reasons for the destruction and the retardation that have befallen these lands.

Countrymen,

We are pleased to see how many of you are now returning home, and that some of you have begun to rebuild your houses. What makes us happier still is the hope that this time you do not build for destruction and do not gather fuel to rekindle the war, which, in the past, has only helped the barbarians lay their hands on the abodes of innocent families. Without such hope we would have suggested that you build in brick and wood rather than stone.

We know that the good progress of your affairs depends on intermixing and assimilation, which results in concord and unity. In spite of all objections and contradictions, we hope that something of this concord will sprout and grow after the abundant rains that are expected early this year. May this rain bring us a season of fertility and help us forget some of the past despair.

We bring good news to the afflicted among you. Humanity's gifts of compassion and sacrifice continue to be offered aplenty via steamships from all corners of the world. God has done to the homeland what a father does to his child. The father, who loves his child and does not seek vengeance, beats the child with one hand to discipline it and uses persuasion with the other to educate it. Similarly, after striking down this country with a heavy hand, God invoked pity toward it in the hearts of do-gooders. His deeds have rendered this city and its compassionate residents a haven for the hard-pressed and a refuge for the miserable. He has linked the old world with the new through issuing and receiving aid. Through His superb providence and high qualities He has warned people so they may turn away from their arrogance and move closer to His exalted and elevated being.

From a patriot

CHAPTER 13

Clarion 8

Beirut, December 14, 1860[1]

More on the Moral Losses of the Homeland

Countrymen,

One of the moral losses that the homeland has suffered is a loss of what we call integrity or self-respect. Many a time we saw some patriot lowering his gaze—especially these days when foreigners mention this topic—not out of cowardice or fear, but out of embarrassment and shame. How often he would apologize for his fellow countrymen's state of affairs, arguing that it is how most people behave in catastrophes. And yet, the denigrator would retort: "This behavior is a natural product of Arab instinct regardless of current circumstances." Perhaps you are of the opinion that such a claim is hard to refute by someone seeking the truth rather than sophistry. But one cannot pass a moral judgment based on anecdotes. Perhaps, once they review our specific circumstances and understand how humiliated we have been generation after generation, those who denigrate us will consider our situation with more integrity and empathy. Had they found themselves in a similarly humiliating situation, they would hardly have marveled at their downfall into a situation as low and demeaning as ours.

May fellow countrymen take note and in the future behave in a way that would pull them out of their ignoble situation and restore their self-respect. This will earn them respect in the eyes of others and gradually erase the traits they have acquired under the influence of recent events. One of these acquired traits is the inability to say what one believes and believe what one hears. A foreigner who reads this might exclaim: "Strange, what does the patriot mean? Before the current unrest, were his compatriots any more truthful to claim the events made them less so? And who would believe the words of an Arab—whether rich, well placed, or of noble origin?" This quip is as obvious as a fire on a hilltop. So how and with what do we argue against people questioning our entire race, even as we observe a correlation between their words and reality, especially if we take the race as a whole?

Perhaps our fellow countrymen are displeased to see us repeat the same allegations we are trying to refute. Once, when I was speaking to a man who thinks little of the Arab race and who dismisses all Arabs as cheating liars without exception or consideration of conscience, the Arab blood in me started to boil. In response to his sharp comments, I exclaimed heatedly that lying and cheating are natural dispositions in all peoples and races, a truism backed by what the Messenger has said: "All people are liars."

I did not leave it at that but added: "If Arabs lie more frequently in number and in quantity compared to other races, it is because they lie spontaneously, without deliberation or prudence, nor with a motive or gain in mind, as is the case with the rest of the things they do." But the lying of other races may be graver than that of the Arabs in terms of gravity and quality. For other races lie deliberately and prudently for their own benefit. It is as if their lies are as masterly executed as their deeds.

It is known that two things hold people from lying: religion and public opinion. If only both were present. As for Arab religions, we do not want to touch this delicate matter for fear of offending the feelings of those who uphold it dearly. It will suffice to ask each person to examine their own religion very closely and see whether it gives them an absolute license to lie, or whether it forbids lying completely, or whether it allows it in certain situations but under special conditions and constraints. We are certain that any religion that allows lying cannot be valid. That is because a true religion is from God, who is the truth and its source, as opposed to lying, which is the work of Lucifer, who is the father of lying and liars. Bear in mind that what some call frivolous, symbolic, or fraudulent lying—what Westerners refer to as "white lies"—is as real and sinister as lying can be. It can even be the fount and precursor to serious deceit, for he who is indifferent to venial sins slowly slips into mortal sins.

As for Arab public opinion, no one can claim that it is opposed to this malicious vice of lying. As our popular street saying goes: "Lies are the salt of men, so shame on the gullible." This saying seems to represent public sentiment in this regard and may be used as proof for what we are arguing. However, in the eyes of the truthful—including nonbelievers—the status of the liar is diminished, whosoever that liar is. As is the case in countries where honesty is highly regarded, those characterized by this vile trait do not deserve to be part of respectable society. They are ostracized because they lack self-respect and a sense of honor.

Now, most of you who are reading this pamphlet will admit that the language of Arabs and their culture—their laws, habits, or social structures, their political relations—may contain more things that foster lying or disrespect for truthfulness than those among non-Arabs. Obviously, sparse honesty increases the propensity to disbelieve, and the words of liars are doubted, even when they speak the truth. It is related that once a shepherd was herding the sheep of his father near his hometown when he cried jokingly, "Wolf! Wolf!" People hurried to help him but did not find a wolf. He did that twice and thrice and the people kept coming for help. But then an actual wolf came by and when the boy called for help, no one rushed to his aid. The wolf devoured him and drove away his sheep.

Truth telling and credulity were scarce before the current unrest in this country and became even more so after it—so much so that one could be forgiven for thinking that we are living in a world of make believe, not reality. And since truth telling and credulity are two essential pillars of comfort, security, and success in business and social conduct, their absence constitutes a grave evil and a great loss.

Let's hope that our people will change the previous saying into "Truth is the salt of men, and shame on the liars!" and stick to the new rendition in word and deed. Otherwise, this patriot himself will be obliged to cite what the Cretan poet and prophet once said to his compatriots, as recorded in the Epistle to Titus, namely that vice, like disease, is pervasive among all peoples and races, and so each distinguished itself by a particular bad trait for which each became known.[2]

Who has traits that are all agreeable?
He is noble whose faults are enumerable

Another moral loss was that of general comfort all over the country. Whoever roams Syrian cities, villages, mountains, and plains these days—especially those places that were the theater of war and transgressions—will only come across extremely depressing scenes, and will only hear whining, complaints, and dissatisfaction with the misery all around. Even more ruin seems to lie ahead in a different garb. It is possible that one of the results of this unrest is the flight of so much money and so many men that the inhabitants left in the country are in such a state of humiliation and want that many of them will turn into impoverished beggars.

True, we see that a house is being built over here, and a plot of land is being ploughed over there, but we fear that every time a private dome is built, a public shrine is torn down. It was said that one day a cat entered a blacksmith's shop, and licked the rasp. It tasted so sweet that the cat kept on licking until he became tongue-less. How miserable and unfortunate Syria is! How few are its means! And how neglectful its people have been! Would Syria not be better off and able to avoid this miserable state if it could get rid of the murderers that constitute the germs of corruption? It is as if this country is doomed with misfortune and backwardness or—as the saying goes—"Under a curse and abetting its own ruin." It is as if whenever Syria takes one step forward it takes several steps backward. Who can fend off fate and destiny?

Another loss was that of trust between one community and another and among members of the same community. Such a loss strips people of their peace of mind and sense of prosperity. It also stands in the way of their progress and success. One abysmal type of this lack of trust—which has very damaging consequences—is the lack of confidence in the rulers and the ruled or between the subjects and their government. It is widely known that the state officials' trust in ordinary people is largely conditional on the people's trust in them and vice versa. Therefore hard work is required from both sides to regain trust and strengthen its foundations.[3]

Let us hope that the heinous effects brought about by the recent events will gradually be alleviated through the corrective actions of ruler and ruled. Rulers need to exercise wisdom, govern with aptitude, and reform their conduct toward their subjects, whom they should respect. Subjects, on the other hand, need to know that their best interest lies in the common good, to exercise forbearance and avoid extremism in seeking a pardon or punishment for what is prohibited politically, religiously, morally, and according to custom. Then, the wheel of trust will eventually spin back to its previous level, based on ties, customs, upbringing, and traits as well as on the common degree of civilization shared between both ruler and ruled.

Another moral loss is that of some people's family honor. Perpetrators of such irreparable loss have surpassed the limits of humanity and gone even further than the savages and barbarians who refrain from heinous acts that are disgusting to the ear and revolting to human nature. Yet another loss is that of many rare books and valuable libraries. In the past, books were saved from the damage of mites, dust, and fire by selling them off cheaply and thus dispensing them to the people. This time around, the hand of cruelty has not exempted books. Nor did the hand of cruelty exempt the herds of animals, not even the silkworm, whose hard labor helps weave clothing to provide for the naked and shield orphans and widows. Finally, we have lost the safety of doing business. Many craftsmen and their practical skills are irreplaceably lost. Who can calculate all this damage to the homeland as well as to the government?

And what about spiritual losses and the corruption of the manners and morals of the public? All of these are hard to miss by the perceptive observers among us. There are other losses that we chose not to mention for brevity's sake or due to their infamy. What we have mentioned in this and the previous two addresses will persuade those who want to believe that wars generate enormous evil and that civil wars are the most evil thing under the sun.

Does it befit us to stand by and look on at these losses with our hands tied only to find ourselves in a state of despair and hopelessness, unable to compensate the loss? Nay, our way forward is to roll up our sleeves, to make a determined effort to conduct our affairs calmly and quietly, and to acquire what grants us peace and success. We need to alleviate the damage and destruction around and within us, while avoiding its causes through self-reflection. The rest is best left to Heavenly Prudence and Self-Sufficient Providence, and to the efforts, acumen, and wisdom of those in charge.

These are the material and moral losses we set out to show. God willing, we will follow this with an inventory of moral gains in order to grant this topic its proper due. May God preserve you.

From a patriot

CHAPTER 14

Clarion 9

January 14, 1861[1]

Moral Gains of the Homeland

Countrymen,

A reader of the title of this pamphlet might stop and wonder: Given this patriot's previous criticism and given the size of the damage and loss incurred by it, are there any benefits at all that the homeland has gained from the civil unrest?

Since in our corrupt world good and evil do not exist in their pure forms and since every matter has two sides—one dark and ugly, the other bright and pleasant—the Syrian affair, too, does have its bright side. So far, we have not exposed our publication's readers to this side except on rare occasions, in passing, or in digressions. Now, we do not want to be accused of being cock-eyed and, like perennial pessimists, of talking only about the dark side of the current affair. Rather, we would like to raise our compatriots' hopes and alleviate some of the depressing effects that the ugly scenes of past events brought about. So we decided to elaborate on what kind of positive side effects the unrest may have generated for the homeland. Potential past and future gains occur as by-products of events rather than as intended outcomes; or—to put it better—they are the workings of Providence. So this is what we say.

One of the moral gains of the latest unrest is our compatriots' concrete realization of the horrors of civil war in their own right as well as in the results they yield. This knowledge should, of course, make them feel deep remorse and genuine regret for what has happened; it should also serve as a deterrent for committing such repulsive acts in the future. Knowledge through personal experience will reinforce these sentiments and expose how senseless such violence is. As the saying goes: "They learn through their pockets." Sooner or later, the issues that have triggered the strife and led people to act the way they did are bound to be put before an official commission and tried for all their implications and consequences. Based on this, people do well to realize that it is better for them to settle conflicts by these permissible, nay politically and religiously sanctioned, means. Allowing disagreements to go beyond the limits of moderation by seeking revenge will only unleash on them more evil destruction, the wrath of the authorities, and the contempt of the civilized world.

Another gain is that fellow countrymen may now realize that their public welfare and by extension their personal well-being require that virtuous ties of unity and concord exist between the different communities and among themselves individually. No wise man can deny that the people of Syria possess the highest quality of mind, natural alertness, and the preparedness for moral and industrial progress toward the highest degrees of civilization. Let those with nefarious intentions and those who are prejudiced against the Syrians say what they may. Syria remains one of the finest countries in terms of its natural strength and commercial centers. The country and its people would not have reached this state of deterioration, humiliation, and backwardness were it not for the lack of unity and paucity of love among Syrians, for their indifference to the welfare of their country and compatriots, for their incredibly foolish surrender to the power of fanaticism, and for the allure of confessional, sectarian, and familial prejudices. Add to that their willingness to be led by the conspiracies and machinations of those who do not care about the welfare of current or future generations. Such people relish the proliferation of differences and enmities among factions and between individuals. In fact, they hold full sway over the hearts of allies and victims alike and make them believe that destroying is preferable to building.

We do not expect that the effects of the recent unrest will disappear in the near future. But we can reasonably hope that sons of the homeland will not forget any time soon the abominable reasons behind the unrest, so that they remain vigilant not to fall into similar predicaments in the future. Let us hope that they have come to value the welfare of their homeland over the fulfillment of harmful and perverted desires and over the lust of those who led and drove them toward that deep-seated hatred and dreadful demise.

Another gain is the growing conviction of our compatriots among others that those despicable wars and terrible atrocities were the logical consequences of irreligious and uncivilized proclivities. Without reforming their ways, they will likely fall deeper into misery, and not recover from their downfall. As long as our people do not distinguish between religion, which is necessarily an intimate matter between the believer and his Creator, and civic affairs, which govern and shape social and political relations between the human being and their fellow countrymen or between them and their government, as long as our people do not draw a sharp line to separate these two distinct concepts, they will fail to live up to what they preach or practice.

Moreover, as long as our compatriots do not open the doors of knowledge and industry and encourage their dissemination among their elites and commoners alike, they should expect neither to join civilized peoples nor to be respected in the eyes of others, or—for that matter—in the eyes of one another. Nor should they presume that the doors to high office in the Ottoman government are open to them. For even though the Arabs were leaders and office holders of the highest reputation in times past, there is no hope in their advancement to anything higher than a scribe, dragoman, council member, or anything similar if they remain in their current condition.

Were our government to adopt a system like that of the Chinese empire, for example, where government positions are restricted to those who are qualified, master the language of their country, and are experts in the laws and organizations of the empire, God knows how many office holders would keep their current positions. Any reasonable person knows how much this country and its people as a whole would gain from the establishment of a meritocratic system akin to the Chinese one. May we see such a system come to being by founding a public college, which would to facilitate the creation of a merit-based bureaucracy, so that both improved education and better government may be counted among the moral gains of the homeland.[2]

For we strongly hope that in the future our compatriots will give culture, morals, and industry their due consideration and expand them among not just men but also women. For the latter are the mothers of the land whose civilization is the greatest blessing and a precondition for our country's success and for the success of its people. Conversely, keeping women uncivilized is one of the greatest curses for the homeland.[3]

Let us also hope that in the future our compatriots will not look at themselves through the lens of sect or race but in terms of merit, virtue, and patriotic brotherhood. Such differences ought not lead to hate, envy, and alienation among our compatriot's different communities any more than differences in personal appearance, natural inclinations, clothes, and daily ways of living invoke envy and dislike among individuals. May they use this diversity, instead, as a means to awaken feelings of healthy competition, enthusiasm, conscientiousness, and kindness. Anyone who compares regions where differences exist to where they do not knows that these healthy feelings are often the outcome of such diversity. Those who have observed the matter closely recognize that when political authority was absent or weak, this diversity has often managed to sustain the cultural strength that prevented further unrest before or while it occurred.

Whoever does not consider this diversity carefully will inevitably wonder why it took so long for the current unrest to erupt rather than be surprised by it. Let us assume the impossible scenario that, ceteris paribus, all Syrians belong to a single group or nation, whether Muslim or Christian. Would this have been a sufficient guarantee to prevent unrest and foreign intervention? Anyone with a sound opinion and the faintest knowledge about peoples' histories and Syria's more recent history cannot help but arrive at the firm conclusion that the decline would have been worse, the destruction even more widespread and terrible, and the danger much graver and uglier.

Another gain of the unrest is that our compatriots have come to realize that they are not alone in the world. They constitute a central rather than peripheral ring in a global chain. This ring holds a highly significant political and religious meaning. Our ring both connects and separates East and West and as such exists in difficult circumstances. Today, with advancements like the telegram and steamships, the rings of this great chain have drawn much closer to one another and become more interdependent. Therefore, unless they wish to face humiliation, defeat, and hatred, it is the duty of all those who were destined to be the intermediaries—such as the Syrians—to avoid provoking their neighbors and to be a steady and cooperative link in this worldwide chain. In this case, the loss will be theirs and no one else's.

Another gain is the realization among intelligent, honorable, and wealthy countrymen that blame, loss, and responsibility ultimately rest with them. They should realize that it is in their best interest to know their limits and to diligently keep the ignorant at bay through education. To promote peace, concord, and amicability by example and instruction will help overcome their opposites. If the wise among Syrians had accounted for the consequences of deeds and realized sooner that developments would lead to the current unrest's far-reaching effect, then they might have expelled the first obsessive whisper that the devil or those with ulterior motives instilled in their minds. They could have immediately smothered the first spark hurled into Syria's parched forests and barren slopes by an ignorant fool or a sly conniver. Even if they could not have managed to extinguish the fire, at least they would have immediately abandoned the thick of war and its foolish proponents. That way, they would have proven to the world that they had no hand in these atrocities and barbaric acts and that they did not approve of them, and that they occurred against both their disposition and their will.

What could the commoners, whose most conspicuous characteristic is ignorance, have done without someone supplying them with money, logistics, and the tools of war? What can one ask of people who are mere instruments in the hands of those in power and who are led by their notables, even against their own interests, assuming that they know what their interests are? It follows that demanding collective punishment for all those who took part in the unrest is no better than blanket impunity. Both are extreme measures, neither religiously nor politically permissible. The former would amount to an act of barbarity, as the entire country would be cleansed of most of its men, given that very few did not participate in one way or another in these events. The latter, meanwhile, would entail the survival of those who are the virus of corruption and the roots of unrest. Setting those people free would boost the morale of evildoers and would expose the country to the perils of falling again into unrest instigated by them.

Another gain is that our fellow countrymen have become persuaded in a tangible way that governance is not only the salt but the very life of the Earth, and that laws exist to constrain evildoers and troubled souls. For lack of governance and the disrespect for the law are two of the worst evils to befall a country, whatever the degree of civilization and success the country has enjoyed. This is because governance and laws are like good health; their worth is only appreciated in their absence.

We hope that, given Syria's pivotal position in the world and the various interests of foreigners in it, Syrians have been persuaded that their transgression of the boundaries of moderation and humanity incurs the blame of the entire world and necessitates foreign intervention. Foreign political intervention may temporarily benefit some individuals, but we strongly believe that it is harmful to all countries. In a country like this one that is home to different races, rife with rooted differences and opposing views regarding foreign intervention, the latter is especially harmful given the different political and religious interests of the intervening powers. However, we maintain that, this time around, the intervention was beneficial to all groups and absolutely necessary to put an end to the spread of unrest and destruction. Both were like an infectious disease spreading with determination and speed from one place to another. We wish that this intervention had taken place earlier or produced its desired effect before things got out of hand and the destruction became so widespread.

The entire Syrian people are indebted to these foreign hands. The latter lent support to their trusted counterparts of the Ottoman state and to the honest among its soldiers, in order to put an end to the unrest and restrain the evildoers behind it who disobeyed God and their rightful rulers. We hope that this foreign assistance, contingent on serving Syria's interest, will continue until the fundamentals of justice and security are irrevocably established and until there is no more reason to fear the aggression, betrayal, and unrest committed by the connivers and their lowly and savage allies in the population.

We also hope that those countrymen who have become civilized will not turn their faces away haughtily from their brethren and alienate themselves in their own country. That is not an act of brotherly patriotism; it bodes ill for the country and hence for our fellow countrymen, particularly for their offspring. Rather, the civilized need to work tirelessly toward the benefit of the homeland and its children, even if they do not immediately reap the fruits of their endeavors and their sacrifices.

Countrymen,

The year 1860 has passed by with all its great incidents and its mystifying turbulences that affected these lands and the rest of the world. In its stead, we welcome the arrival of a new political year and hope that it will be one of comfort, affluence, and security in Syria and for its people. Given the calamities that shook the world last year, we cannot but hope that the fallout does not last beyond the end of this year. May the latter be a better one marked by rebuilding and peacefulness.

To fulfill these hopes, we have to remind our compatriots of two important issues. First, healing their country and fixing their lot depend on unity and personal diligence. This is because depending on others is like a hungry man who thinks his hunger will subside when his friend or his lord eats, or like an ignorant man who relies on the education of his neighbor or coreligionist to become a philosopher. For whoever cannot stand on their own cannot rely on anyone to prop them up.

Second, showing hatred toward the whole of society based on the sins that some of its members committed either consciously or carelessly is not only unfair but also harmful, as it prevents the very unity and concord upon which the success of the people and the country depends. We hardly need to remind our countrymen that regret and remorse should be met with the spirit of forgiveness. This can bring hearts closer together and help restore concord. This is what the good neighbor and the true brother seek in our homeland; without concord success is elusive for neighbors and brothers even though their personal and professional interests are so intertwined.

May God guide the leaders and decision makers toward the good of everyone and the comfort of the public, and may He grant them the will and ability to achieve that. May God preserve you.

From a patriot

CHAPTER 15

Clarion 10

February 22, 1861[1]

More on the Moral Gains of the Homeland

Countrymen,

One of the moral gains of the homeland that resulted from the recent unrest is becoming aware of many issues. First of all, the rulers realize they need to attend more closely to their reign in order to be able to anticipate problems before they occur and not to neglect them lest they become too overwhelming to solve. Had the initial perpetrator of the crime been punished, or the landed tax farmer or district officer where the first murder had taken place been held responsible, it would have served as a lesson and deterrent for others. Such actions would have been one of the best ways to end incitement before it spread and deepened. However, if no one is held accountable for the murders or if the murderer falls into the hands of authorities and they dismiss the case through money, reconciliation, or temporary imprisonment, then life becomes expendable and bloodletting inconsequential for those with evil and corrupt intentions. They would commit more crimes and atrocities; matters would only get worse until the entire the country and its people are once again ruined.

Second, rulers and governors need to be faithful to the state, the country, and the people. These rulers must be qualified and strong-willed; they must be capable personally and militarily to impose legislations and discipline on the wrongdoers, while steering clear of sowing the kind of divisions through their action that have been handed down from darker ages. Of course, agitators and corrupt hoodlums exist in every age, period, and country. But it saddens us to say that the permissiveness and extreme lenience on the part of the government in our country have increased their numbers in the hinterland. Their existence prevents the country from enjoying a sense of ease, security, and success.

Third, the will of the sultan and his sublime authority needs to be carried out. Ottoman subjects in all communities ought to give him his due respect on religious and political grounds. They should not challenge him, nor should any official of any rank dodge or ignore implementing his eminent ordinances. It is no secret that the imperial decrees that are issued by him, whom God has granted the throne of the sultanate, are intended for the comfort of the people, the prosperity of their livelihood, and the security of their income. If his decrees were tailored to the various whims and prejudices of local officials, they would lose their binding sense for some and imply preferential treatment for others. This is why either imperial decrees should be totally revoked in the same way they were promulgated, i.e., publicly, or they should be applied in full to reflect the letter of their issuer's will. The former hypothetical revocation is impossible; the latter is a duty and a necessity. For anyone who is not blinded by prejudice and deafened by fanaticism is aware that half-hearted implementation of the decrees will shake the foundations of the law, confuse the people, foster disagreement among them, and obstruct their commercial and other transactions. It will simply place everyone in a state of suspicion or illusion.

Fourth, authority needs to be delegated based on merit and qualification, not on nationality or family lineage, wealth or high social status. In today's world, the most successful and progressive empires are those that observe this principle, which applies to spiritual as well as political office. The reason is this: anyone who counts on being promoted to higher ranks by virtue of birthright or by belonging to a certain race, tribe, or lineage that rose to a privileged status thanks to fate, the ignorance of past generations, or the activity and toil of its founding father is unlikely to exert the efforts necessary for the evolution and progress of those who do not yet enjoy the honorable privilege he forged for himself.

This is especially the case if they belong to the fourth generation or thereafter of a noble lineage. Being so distant from the founder of a family's glory, their attributes lag far behind those of their forefathers—much as an imitator lags behind an inventor. They also lose and belittle the traits necessary to preserve his and their glory because they succumb to the illusion that what their forebears built was not the fruit of long and hard work but, rather, some self-evident reality. It follows that latter generations become aloof. They develop a sense of scorn toward others and entitlement over them with little regard to their welfare. If it so happened that some of the founder's qualities are still in them, they would be in a state of decline and degeneration.[2] They would not be worthy of the position they hold, nor could they rise to their tasks. It is one's heart and speech, not origin, that determines one's worth. Would it not be ideal if one possessed both, merit and noble descent?

Fifth, it is necessary to erect a barrier between leadership or spiritual authority, on the one hand, and politics or civil authority, on the other. This is because the former is linked—by itself and by nature—to interior and fixed matters that do not change with time and circumstance, whereas the latter is related to external matters that are not fixed but can change and be reformed depending on place, time, and circumstance. The two are distinct and incompatible. It is well nay impossible to reconcile both in one person. Without separating both types of authority, it is no exaggeration to say that no civilization can exist, live, or grow.

Given their distinct and contradictory spheres of action, combining both can lead to many negative consequences. It will harm and undermine religious creeds as well as political deliberations. Each authority would annul the other's effects and benefits, which, when applied correctly, would supply the best means to serve the intended recipient of both authorities, that is, their shared subject: the human being on the inside in relation to religion and on the outside in relation to politics. Combining both authorities can also encourage many to pursue spiritual office not out of love but out of greed for the temporal privileges, civil authority, and sway that the position undeservedly bestows on them. Conversely, matters of political nature could be handed over to those whose temperaments are ill suited or who were not educated to handle such tasks. Politicians need to be aware of the specificities of their surroundings and the concrete laws governing them. Spiritual leaders, by contrast, are trained in meditation of the mind and abstract judgment, which are necessarily removed from the specific circumstances of a certain object, an individual, a generation, a nation, or type of people.

Since politics has a strong hold on the self and its temperament, it can distract these people from performing the duties ordained by their spiritual office. Spiritual duties are in themselves sublime; they are more virtuous, important, and honorable since they are directed toward the better part of the human being, the inner self. The dereliction of their ordained duty results in the people's loss of faith in religion. They start acting like sheep without a shepherd. They refrain from honing their political craftsmanship and rely instead on the judgment of their spiritual leaders. These leaders only seem to agree to disagree, and if they happen to agree, their agreement is only at face value, short-lived, and inconsequential. This is how differences between their leaders become essential and then eternally entrenched among the people. We do not single out leaders of a specific sect. Rather we speak of the leaders of all the many sects of our country: Muslims, Christians, Druze, ʿAlawis, Ismaʿilis, Yazidis, Jews, and Samaritans, not to mention their various schools of thought and their offshoots.

Civilized countries have long realized the damage resulting from combining the two authorities. They have drawn a clear line between the spiritual and political realms, not allowing the one to interfere in the interests of the other. The stronger the separation, the greater the success and peace of mind. There is no doubt that this separation should also please legitimate spiritual leaders. It relieves them of many temporal burdens and from their pangs of conscience since political preoccupation unavoidably leads to negligence of the spiritual duties to which they dedicated their lives and teachings. Now, should this separation and the measures it entails be carried out gradually or abruptly? That depends not only on place, time, existing mood, and circumstance, but also on the informed opinion and the judicious will of those entitled to rule.

Sixth, it is necessary to take strong, effective measures to completely secure people's most cherished goods, as well as their trade, skills, and knowledge. Whoever compares the successful cultivation of the many fertile plains in Syria with its rocky and hard-to-plough mountains realizes the virtue of security. It makes all the difference as to whether a fertile plain turns arid or fertile. And whoever compares Syria's current ratio of harvests to population to that of ancient times will notice that its productivity, the wealth of its people, and its government can be increased manifold based on its natural resources. Given the current security deficit, the impoverishment of the people, and the injustices of the governors and local rulers, today's unusually low agricultural production is no surprise.

Eighth *[sic]*, rulers and regional governors need to look after their subjects, and care for the worthy among them. They need to maintain their subjects' comfort, well-being, and professional success. There is no doubt that this conduct will increase the love and trust that subjects hold toward their rulers. It will also convince the subjects not to place their commerce and interests under foreign control and protection. All of this is more obvious than a fire on a hilltop.

Countrymen,

We have thus enumerated the moral gains even though we and other compatriots wish they had not come at such cost and damage to the homeland. There are many other gains we did not dwell on because they either were referred to previously, or are self-evident, or are related to the future, which makes them near impossible to anticipate or predict. Despite the ongoing trepidation, unrest, and fragmentation, we still hope that these thick clouds will be followed, God willing, by ample rain and bountiful harvests. Through the perseverance of its guardians, a new era will dawn upon Syria. Signs of this age and its advancing armies can be discerned from the imminent opening of the carriage way, the introduction of railway lines, and the expansion of schools and hospitals.[3]

How we wish to see our compatriots, spiritual leaders, and political rulers compete constructively to contribute to these works! We believe that they are capable of it. Moreover, we wish that foreigners, who want to contribute to the welfare of the country rather than their own self-interest, follow the example of those who know best about this country and its people and thereby teach the countrymen in the language of the country. Using Arabic as a language of instruction benefits the language itself. On the one hand it makes the educated more productive and compassionate toward their country, on the other it makes them more acceptable to their fellow countrymen. Those who claim it is not possible to advance on the ladder of civilization using the Arabic language may not realize the merits of this language. Its reform is more feasible and effective than the attempt to civilize Arabs using various foreign languages. Otherwise, we will have to accept regretfully and gloomily that Syria is also bound to become the Babel of languages, customs, and ideologies on top of being the Babel of religions, races, and confessions that it already is.

Countrymen,

You have been well known for generosity, gallantry, zeal, alertness, chivalry, and tolerance. You are now riding the wave of the nineteenth century's generation of knowledge and illumination, of invention and discovery, of culture and learning, of arts and crafts, of progress and civilization.[4] Do not let those intense seditious acts of civil war lead you away from these good traits of yours. Rather, you should rise up, be aware and awake, and roll up your sleeves of verve and vigor.

Behold morals and civilization, means of unity and concord hailing from every direction crowding your doors, knocking with might and urgency, demanding entry into your adorned and coveted cities, your proud mountains, your valleys, deserts, and plains, which nature has so beautifully arranged with all its pleasant ornaments and dazzling power. So rid yourselves of your religious fanaticisms, confessional factionalism, sectarian enmities, and selfish prejudices! Open the gates to such noble guests like morals and civilization. Welcome them, extend them a united hand to shake, and accept them with delight and joy. It will fill your country with comfort, prosperity, and peace and cover your quarters with happiness, elegance, and pride.

From a patriot

CHAPTER 16

Clarion II

April 22, 1861[1]

On Civilization

Countrymen,

We have touched upon the issue of civilization many times in our previous pamphlets. Since many people of this generation are preoccupied with this topic, and since the spirit of the age is strongly inclined toward seeking it, and reaping its fruits, many are in danger of falling victim to false assumptions about the concept. They tend to mistake fake as well as traditional forms of civilization for the real thing. They remain content with the former as opposed to pursuing the latter, having convinced themselves that they maintain a firm grip on it. In reality, they are still very far from it. Therefore, we have decided to explain to our compatriots briefly what civilization is and how it is attained.

Let us not delve into its benefits and pleasures for now. There is no time, and no need given the overwhelming tendency to believe in its enjoyments. Instead, we will argue the following: Civilization originally comes from the word *city*. This derivation can either be based on the distinction between city and nomadic desert or village and countryside. In the first instance, civilization refers to the lifestyle of sedentary people as opposed to the lifestyle of nomads, who know no civilization. In the second instance, its contradistinction to the village refers to the city's comfortable lifestyle, architectural order, and the like, which city dwellers erroneously claim are absent in the countryside among peasants and villagers.[2]

The concept of civilization has been expanded since then to mean inward and outward cultivation of the self and the attainment of knowledge, culture, and virtue. It is no secret that in this world man is in one of two states: one of wilderness and barbarity, or one of civilization and grace. The state of barrenness is the natural state into which man is born. If he stays in it, there is little difference between him and dumb animals and the damage he causes would be greater than that of animals. As for the state of civilization, it is a consequence of the gradual cultivation in manners and morals through emulation, hard work, and diligence. Only those with a proclivity toward these attributes reach their highest form.

The relation of wild humans to civilized humans is often presented as the relation of the ignorant to the wise, the animal to the human, darkness to light, and the blind to the seeing. It appears like the relation of monstrous flesh-eaters in distant Africa to the notables and dignitaries of Paris and England or the relation of desert Arabs to those living in Beirut. But contrary to such representations, civilization can be superficial and fake when based on the imitation and appropriation of certain foreign characteristics, customs, and habits rather than on fundamental, real, and contemporary principles. The bearer of this type of civilization resembles a drum—great in size and sound but hollow on the inside and totally unusable after the slightest damage. His relation to true civilization is like a shadow's relation to a body, or illusion's relation to reality. As for true civilization, in a nutshell, it is that universal state of society that suits the development of all the forces of the human race, individually and collectively.

Civilization is, therefore, not confined to a single thing or to particular forms of knowledge among the populace, such as sciences or trades, for example. Rather, its essential end being development, it includes all sorts of affairs organized in a social structure. Subject to certain connections, civilization starts with the human being's inner self and then extends outward. The primary objective of civilization is growth. For the success of humans does not rest on the accumulation of personal wealth— whatever this wealth may be. Instead, it rests on the growth and expansion of their faculties and their appropriate use according to the original purpose for which they were meant. Humans were not created in the form of a sponge that absorbs all it can from the world's material wealth but, rather, in the image of an ever-growing, fruit-bearing tree. Nor do their success, virtue, and happiness rest on the wealth and knowledge they have accumulated and acquired for themselves. Instead, it rests on the useful deeds they can bring to bear on society. As the poet says:

> Whoever does no good in someone else's name
> To me, his presence or absence is the same.

Based on the previous definition, it is clear that the mission and meaning of true civilization remain incomplete if they do not aid in the overall development and progress, both materially and morally, of humans. This is because the nurture of one's body alone reduces him to an animal; the nurture of body and mind less the morals reduces him to the devil incarnate; and the nurture of mind alone makes of him a possible contributor to world ruin and the total fading out of the human race. True civilization, then, looks at each of those forces—body, mind, and culture—with a balanced perspective and gives them their appropriate attention according to their relative standing and virtue. This is to be done by rewarding the most virtuous with virtue and the most vicious with vice, both collectively and individually. We say so for the following reasons.

First, true civilization elevates a people by elevating each member one by one—men as well as women. Second, true civilization is not concerned with one segment of the populace to the exclusion of another but places everyone on an equal footing. Now, if we compare the previous definition of civilization to how it was practiced by Greeks, Romans, and Arabs of past generations, we observe two shortcomings: these civilizations did not cultivate all the different aspects of the individual, and civilization was not present among all its peoples. It was like a house without a roof or a vault without the pivotal stone. It was hence of little use, short-lived, and with meager benefits for current generations.

Likewise, if we examine Europe's current civilization in light of this definition, we see that it is lacking in many ways. Many bearers of progress there seek their own private good, and guard their power and privilege more than they care for the development of knowledge and culture among their people. Thus, we see over there knowledge, kindness, and discipline next to ignorance, vulgarity, cruelty, drunkenness, and excessive self-love, not to mention obscene customs. For regardless of how eminent and glamorous a given civilization appears, only adhering to the healthy principles of common sense will put it on the right path. Otherwise its existence will be troubled and short, and its sway weak and poor.

As for Syria, we were proud that before last year's unrest, the country had set its left foot on the first step of the ladder of civilization. We were hopeful that it would, in a short time, reach the highest echelons. As for now, we have no other recourse than to cover our mouth with our hands and await what future days and God's Providence hold in store for us.

Countrymen,

Anything precious in this life is susceptible to imitation and forgery. The more precious and desired it is, the more efforts forgers make to reproduce a copy and present it to the public as genuine. The same way commodities, foodstuffs, and medicine are forged, so, too, is the precious and sought-after commodity that is civilization. We see our present generation in clear danger of adopting, for various reasons, a brand of civilization that neither merits the name nor bears the fruits of true civilization. This generation is so heavily dependent on this fake form that we fear that it may become too content with it, thereby stalling success.

Westerners have collectively attained great levels of civilization, higher than that achieved by Easterners, including the children of these lands that, in times passed, produced the cradle of civilization, centers of knowledge and glamour. It is thus feared that many of our compatriots who are more inclined toward imitation and more capable of it will be content with mimicking Western customs, clothes, and traits. For everything foreign is enjoyable and everything new is alluring, and our era is dominated by the West, whose customs and taste hold more sway than those of the East. Those who engage in such mimicry are under the illusion that their conduct suffices to mark them as civilized and to have them regarded in higher esteem than their own kin and countrymen. What they are oblivious to is that such imitation makes them strangers in the eyes of their compatriots and despicable imposters of customs, unworthy of the clothes they wear, in the eyes of foreigners.

Like any reasonable person, we would not dispute that acquiring good qualities from wherever in the world is desirable, or that many of the benefits of civilization come from the West and many people of Europe deserve full respect. We nevertheless cannot blindly take for granted that everything coming to us from there is in itself useful and compatible with the good progress of Easterners, who, like all people, are fundamentally shaped by their country's atmosphere. Those who are willing to clutch at anything that comes their way from Europe without precise examination, sound criticism, and the strict selection of what is useful in terms of progress and refinement on par with Westerners are fooling themselves. They do not distinguish much between a forged dirham and a genuine dinar. They are patching up worn clothes with new rags. That is how people are.

It is no secret that anyone who shuns anything Western solely for being Western and applauds anything Arab solely for being Arab, or vice versa, falls into harmful extremism. People are naturally more inclined toward exterior rather than inner matters. They clutch more at appearance than at essence—especially regarding things like science and religion that require intensity of thought, prudent contemplation, and sharp inquiry. People apply themselves to the matter of civilization in a similar manner. They think that civilization is based on lifestyle, the way houses are laid out, how exquisite clothes are, eating at a table, making polite conversation, mixing of women and men, the acquisition of a foreign language, and the like. Overall, these practices have no benefit other than damage to people's character and personal virtues that set them apart as members of a notable and chosen community. In fact, such matters are the mere leaves or the bark of civilization. They are the most immaterial outcomes and least useful benefits. They are foreign fruits suspended temporarily on the tail end of the tree of civilization. As a poet once said:

> Do not be impressed by a man's attire.
> About his manners you must inquire!
> Were it not for the fragrance a branch emits
> The difference between branches and firewood would not exist.

Countrymen,

Many means of civilization have been elucidated in previous pamphlets. Some are more important than others. The first of those is religion. We do not mean any religion. Rather, we mean true religion as revealed from God. True religion is the foundation of true civilization. The freer this religion is from impurities bound to seep into every aspect of people's lives, the purer the civilization that results from it is. Furthermore, any religion that holds ignorance as the father of faith and stupidity as the mother of piety cannot serve as a sound foundation for civilization.

The second is political authority. We do not mean any type of authority. Rather, our reference is to government concerned with the welfare of its subjects, their prosperity, their professional success, and their progress in knowledge, wealth, and civilization. In this sense political authority becomes a model that offers strong and effective measures to spread civilization among them. Whoever has noticed the strong connection and relationship between government and subjects will agree with us that no civilized people survive under uncivilized rule. Conversely, no civilized rule is possible over an uncivilized people because the two are intertwined. How true rings the adage "You get the government you deserve."

The third is the means of acquiring cultural morals, such as schools, printing houses, newspapers, commerce, and the like, which bring people closer together like one family. Whatever the means to civilization, it is agreed upon that individuals and peoples acquire it gradually rather than in one fell swoop. The easier it is for the people to access these means and the more widespread they are among its elites and commoners, the stronger, faster, firmer, and more practical civilization becomes.

Countrymen,

We believe that two factors, frequently mentioned in our previous patriotic tracts, are essential today to civilizing our compatriots: The first one is concord among them as individuals and groups. This is especially the case regarding civic concord, whose existence or lack thereof depend more on the strength, activity, and will power of authorities than on the whims of ordinary people and their various biases. As for heartfelt religious concord, it surprises us little that it has become difficult, if not impossible, to attain after what happened and given the fatal stagnation that has gripped our homeland's religions and laws.

The second factor is love of the homeland in general, and placing its interest ahead of selfish ones, whether personal or sectarian, in particular. As long as our compatriots do not feel that this is their homeland and their country, there is no hope that they love it or care for its welfare. Rather, they would always be disunited, each one seeking what they imagine is useful to them or to their faction.

It is well known that any house or piece of property that is divided is doomed for destruction. Therefore, relying on the wishes and opinions of Syrians to fix the situation in the country is like asking for the impossible or like expecting the sick and the guilty to heal and judge themselves. Even if we were to acknowledge that Syrians know their own good, we cannot assume that they all agree on it. Furthermore, if they decided to agree, there is little hope that they will be allowed to enjoy it. Hence, this country is heading in an extremely dangerous direction. There is no hope for this country's reconstruction or salvation from ruin, unless God guides its people into the right direction, or, through His extraordinary providence, supplies effective and unprejudiced means to civilization, or at least puts it on the path to safety and success.

We cannot do anything now except bemoan this unfortunate country, a country that has become victim to such divergent prejudices and personal interests and home to so few patriots . . .

May God preserve you.

From a patriot

NOTES

INTRODUCTION

1. Makdisi 2000b, 2004; Sheehi 2000, 2004, 2012; Hill 2015a.

2. All issues are preserved in the archive of the American University of Beirut and have been edited in Bustani 1990e.

3. Abkarius 1920; Mishaqa 1988; al-Ustawani 1994.

4. Nick Danforth, "The Long Sectarian Peace," www.washington-post.com/opinions/the-middle-easts-long-sectarian-peace/2015/04/17/70e015a4-e3b2–11e4–81ea-0649268f729e_story.html.

5. Khalidi 2002: 153–64.

6. On the Crusades, see Ibn al-Jawzi breaking the news of the sacking of Jerusalem in Baghdad in 1099: "How dare you slumber in the shade of complacent safety, leading lives as frivolous as garden flowers, while your brothers in Syria have no dwelling place save the saddles of camels and the bellies of vultures? Blood has been spilled! Beautiful young girls have been shamed! . . . Shall the valorous Arabs resign themselves to insult, and the valiant Persians accept dishonour?" On Arabic responses to the fall of Baghdad, see Haarmann 2002.

7. Indeed, as Armitage (2015) posits, "Every Great Revolution is a Civil War."

8. McCarthy 2015; Krämer 2006; Horne 1977.

9. Mitchell 1988.

10. al-Jabarti 1993; Khalidi 2004: 37; Tageldin 2011: 39–55. Colla 2003.

11. Zurayk 1948/1956.

12. Zurayk 1948/1956; and al-'Azm 1967/2011.

13. Michel Foucault, quoted in Armitage 2012: 500.

14. Makdisi 2000b. See also Rodogno 2012: 91–117.

15. Marx 1968: 398–400.

16. See also Farah 2000.

17. Marx 1968: 400.

18. Djaït 1989. Bustani also used to terms *haraka* (movement, unrest) and *hawadith* (events) to refer to the civil war in 1860.

19. *Nafir Suriyya 5*, November 1, 1860. According to Armitage (2015: 59), the concept of civil war was a Roman invention. *Bellum civile* differed from "*staseis,* the various forms of sedition and rebellion that divided the Greek *polis.*" See also Makdisi 2015.

20. Sarmiento 2004.

21. See, for example, *al-Muqtataf* 8 (1883): 1–7; Salim al-Bustani, "al-Mu'allim Butrus al-Bustani faqid al-watan," *Al-Jinan* 14 (1883): 321–22. Bustani's life and work is discussed later.

22. ElShakry 2013.

23. Tarazi 1913: 70. The Bustanis refused to relaunch it after an official pardon by the sultan.

24. Jeha 2004; ElShakry 2013.

25. Makdisi 2019.

26. Kesrouany 2015; Hill 2015a; Issa 2017.

CHAPTER I

1. Hakim 2013.

2. Winter 2010: 137–38.

3. Barbir 1980; Philipp 2002.

4. al-Yaziji 2002. The first book edition (Harisa, 1936) was titled *Risala tarikhiyya fi ahwal Lubnan fi 'ahdihi al-iqta'i.* See Abu Husayn 1991.

5. al-Bustani 1997.

6. Salibi 1988: 115.

7. For a useful summary of Fakhr al-Din II's political and commercial operations, see Traboulsi 2007: 5–9.

8. Havemann 1983.

9. Havemann 1983, 95–123.

10. Hakim 2013: 22.

11. Cf. Makdisi 2008a: 32–47.

12. Carne 1826: 278–79.

13. Chevallier 1971.

14. Makdisi 2000b: 54.

15. See *Nafir Suriyya 5* (November 1, 1860). On the Antilyas Pact, see also Hourani 1983: 61; and Havemann 1983.

16. Hakim 2013: 37–44.

17. Hakim 2013: 42, 47–49.

18. Makdisi 2000b. As we shall argue later, however, sectarianism was not an actors' category at the time, and there was not yet a name for it.

19. Makdisi 2000b: 97, 2000a.

20. Fawaz 1994: 50; Farah 2000: 542–65; Makdisi 2000b: 211.

21. Fawaz 1994: 68.

22. Farah 2000: 566–82.

23. Hakim 2013: 88. Hakim argues further (2013: 83–87) that the French general's most enduring legacy was perhaps a map he commissioned that was supposed to demonstrate to the concert of Europe that the geographical boundaries of Lebanon extended far beyond even the previous Maronite church's ambit into the Bekaʿ Valley in the east, al-Kabir River in the north, and Bilad Bishara in the south.

24. Makdisi 2000b: 144, 151, 157.

25. Lord Dufferin quoted in Hakim 2013:76.

26. *Nafir Suriyya 1* (September 29, 1860): "Neither the victorious party nor anyone else should assume that the states came to take the side of one group over another, or to protect a certain group or avenge another just because they are Christian or non-Christian. Rather, as far as we know they came only to protect the rights of man *[huquq al-insan]*."

CHAPTER 2

1. Hourani 1983; Khuri 1995; Sheehi 2004; Makdisi 2004, 2008a; Daghir 2008; Bou Ali 2013; Beshara 2014; Sacks 2015; Hanssen and Weiss 2016.

2. Khuri 1995: 9–10; and Mulhim I. al-Bustani, *al-Salsabil* 1968, quoted in Georgescu 1978: 44–46.

3. The Dibbieh branch of the Bustanis had acquired a reputation as a family of Maronite priests and bishops: 'Abdallah Bustani (1780–1866) was the bishop of Tyre, his brother Butrus (1819–99) was bishop of Saida.

4. Zachs 2004: chap. 1.

5. Antonius 1939: 47.

6. Born in Shuwayfat, Khuri's Greek Orthodox family moved to Beirut in 1845, where he studied with Nasif al-Yaziji before teaching for the missionaries at 'Abayh. In 1858, he founded Beirut's first Arabic newspaper, *Hadiqat al-Akhbar,* and the Suriyya printing press. Privately funded and pro-Ottoman in outlook, its editor subsequently enjoyed a long career in the provincial administration and as a poet, most notable for his *al-'Asr al-jadid* (1863), a collection of Hazlittian character poems of prominent figures of the day, first serialized in *Hadiqat al-Akhbar.* For a biography, see Zachs 2004: 27–39.

7. Hanssen 2005a.

8. Tibawi 1963: 155.

9. Jandora 1981: 19.

10. Jessup 1910: 484. See also See Khuri 1995: 14.

11. Tibawi 1963: 158.

12. Abkarius 1920: 70–72.

13. Lindner 2014: 49. Love and equality were key concepts in both *Nafir Suriyya* and later Salim al-Bustani's serialized romantic novels. See Sheehi 2004; Sacks 2015; Holt 2017.

14. Booth 2002: 433–38.

15. Lindner 2014: 55.

16. Eli Smith feared that al-Bustani was not cut out for religious duties that a ministry would entail. He considered him secular in disposition, intelligent, and with an accountant's mind. See Zachs 2004: 223.

17. American Board of Commissioners for Foreign Missions (ABCFM), Houghton Library.

18. The Native Church as it was called counted nineteen male and four female members. Tibawi 1963: 121; Makdisi 2008a: 190.

19. The Bible translation was completed by Cornelius van Dyck and Yusuf al-Asir and published in New York in 1868. See Issa 2017; Grafton 2016; and Binay and Leder 2012.

20. Rahil bore at least eight children: the eldest, Sarah (1844–66), was a teacher and administrator at her father's "National School"; Salim (1846 or 1848–84) worked closely on all his father's educational and editorial projects, became a municipal councilor for Zokak al-Blat, and one of the foundational Arabic novelists. Saʿad was a teacher; Najib was a lawyer, who along with his younger brothers, Amin (a merchant who eventually left for the United States) and Nasib (who died in Egypt), continued editing the family's periodicals and encyclopedias after his father's and older brother's deaths. Adelaide (b. 1849 or 1850) and Alice (1870–1926) achieved recognition for their serialized romance novels, *Hanri wa Imilya* and *Riwaya Sabiʿa* in their father's *al-Jinan.* Holt 2014: 234–35; Hayek 2013; Zachs 2011.

21. They were *Majmaʿ al-tahdhib* and *Jamʿiyya suriyya lil-iktisab al-ʿulum wa al-funun.* See al-Bustani 1990e: 6. In spring 1860, Bustani cofounded with Husayn Bayhum the group Literary Committee for the Spread of Arabic Books *(al-ʿUmda al-adabiyya li-ishhar al-kutub al-ʿarabiyya)* and in 1867 the Syrian Scientific Society *(al-Jamʿiyya al-ʿilmiyya al-suriyya).*

22. For a more complete list of his publications, see the reference list.

23. Bustani 1990f: 45.

24. For the most extensive treatment of this affair, see Makdisi 2008a: chap. 5.

25. His youngest brother, Faris al-Shidyaq (1804–87), who had himself converted to Protestantism and later to Islam, was the exception in the family. From his voluntary exile in Europe, he denounced the Roman Catholic Church in 1855.

26. Makdisi 2008a: 180.

27. In it, Sultan Abdülmecid extended "guarantees . . . to all the subjects of my empire, without distinction of classes or of religion, for the security of their persons and property, and the preservation of their honor, are today confirmed and consolidated, and efficacious measures shall be taken in order that they may have their full entire effect." Hurewitz 1975: 315.

28. Abu-Manneh 1980.

29. Butrus al-Bustani, *Khutba fi adab al-'Arab* (1859). The text is reprinted in Daya 1981.

30. Bustani, *Nafir Suriyya* 6 (November 8, 1860).

31. *Muhit al-Muhit* (Beirut, 1869/70), *Qutr al-Muhit,* 2 vols. (1869), and the first six of *Da'irat al-Ma'arif,* 11 vols. (Beirut, 1876–1900).

32. ABCFM, 16.8.1, *Syrian Mission,* vol. 5, "Annual Report of the Beirut Station for 1863" (Microfilm Reel 545).

33. ABCFM, 16.8.1, *Syrian Mission,* vol. 5, "Annual Report of the Beirut Station for 1863" (Microfilm Reel 545). See also Hanssen 2005a.

34. Khuri 1995: 58.

35. Daniel Bliss to his wife Abby, January 6, 1874, in Bliss 1993: 185.

36. Butrus al-Bustani, "al-Madrasa al-wataniyya," *al-Jinan,* 4 (1873): 627. For more on this school and its pupils who became Nahdawis in their own right, see Hanssen 2005a.

37. In Arabic: *al-Jam'iyya al-'ilmiyya al-suriyya.*

38. Tibawi 1963: 179.

39. Holt 2013: 236.

40. For example, al-Suwaidi 2003. Similar gardens mushroomed in eighteenth-century Istanbul and nineteenth-century Cairo, where leisure classes celebrated them in poetry and as *flâneurs.* See Hamadeh 2008; and Behrens Abouseif 1992.

41. Holt 2009.

42. Hourani 1990. The Egyptian Khedive Isma'il bought one thousand copies and donated a library to al-Bustani. See Choueiri 2003: 64. For two immanent critiques of al-Bustani's lexicographical project, see Sacks 2015: 77–117; and Bou Ali 2012.

43. Issa 2017.

44. Daghir 2008: 128; Bou Ali 2012: 36.

CHAPTER 3

1. al-Bustani 1929; Suwaya 1963.

2. Antonius 1939: 49–50. Antonius's ascription of *Nafir Suriyya* as a weekly publication is misleading. They were in all likelihood posted on Beirut's walls and handed out in intervals of two or sometimes four or more weeks. Antonius suggests that *Nafir Suriyya* was a precursor

to a series of anti-Ottoman announcements posted anonymously on Beirut's walls in 1878. On this affair, see Steppat 1972. We found no information about *Nafir Suriyya*'s readership in the 1860s.

3. Hourani 1983: 101–2. For a critique of the "Arabization" of education in multilingual Bild al-Sham, see Daghir 2008: chap. 2.

4. On the challenge of the *Nahda*'s translation movement to religious certainty and the secularizing function of al-Bustani's "doubt," see Daghir 2008: 51–61. Note though that anthropocentrism is not the same as the secularization thesis (Sachs 2015: 93–94).

5. Sacks 2015: 89.

6. Tibawi 1963: 170–71.

7. Sharabi 1970.

8. Abu-Manneh 1980: 300.

9. For another Syrianist view, see Daya 1981; on the history of the term *Syria* and its revival in the nineteenth century, see Abu-Manneh's student, Fruma Zachs 2005: 245–51.

10. Khuri 1995. See also al-Qays 2005.

11. Makdisi 1997.

12. Makdisi 2004: 608.

13. Fawaz (1994) brings out this point eloquently. As the late Halil Inalcik (1973) reminded us long ago, the eruption of communal violence in the mid-nineteenth century was an effect of the Tanzimat application across the Ottoman empire.

14. Hakim 2013: 71. See also Makdisi 2000b: 147.

15. The term *al-ʿilla* means "source" or "cause." For example, in a lecture at the Syrian Society of Arts and Sciences around 1848, John Wortabet lists the "cause and effect" *(al-ʿilla wa al-maʿlul)* of science taking hold in "Syria." According to Bustani's *Muhit al-Muhit* dictionary (539), *dhamma,* among other things, means "to bring something close," "to associate with."

16. Makdisi 2008a: 599.

17. Ottoman Orientalism is a paradoxical formation: on the one hand, Ottomans internalized and emulated Western notions of civilization, time, and progress. On the other, they were committed to restraining European colonialism, maintaining Ottoman sovereignty, and asserting imperial mastery over the empire's far-flung provinces and regions beyond. See Makdisi 2002.

18. Makdisi 2004: 604.

19. Makdisi 2008a: 199–207.

20. *Nafir Suriyya* 8. For an English translation of al-Bustani's *Khutba,* see Sheehi in El-Ariss 2018: 5–13.

21. Sheehi 2004: 51.

22. For a sociospatial analysis of late Ottoman Beirut, see Hanssen 2005b.

23. Hill 2015a.

24. Kesrouany 2015; Bou Ali 2013: 266. For capitalism and the *Nahda,* see Sheehi 2012.

25. Bou Ali 2013: 267. Benedict Anderson's idea that print capitalism and newspaper culture were indispensable preconditions for the spread of nationalism inspired many studies of Arab nationalisms in the past three decades—so much so that one scholar has labeled this trend the "Beirut School," in reference to the name of the AUB library, which holds the archive of early Arabic newspapers: Khalidi, Anderson, et al. 1991: ix.

26. Bou Ali 2013: 271–73.

27. Holt 2017: 41–84.

28. Holt 2017: 40.

29. Sacks 2015.

30. The call is attributed to Ibrahim al-Yaziji (1847–1910) and is also quoted in the front matter of Antonius's *The Arab Awakening.*

31. Sacks 2015: 9, 78–79, 85, 93, 112.

CHAPTER 4

1. At the end of issue 5, "the sweet sound of the patriot's clarion [was] drowned out by the crude drumbeat of prejudices," while in the final issue of *Nafir Suriyya,* the Arab imitator of Western "civilization resembles a drum—great in size and sound but hollow on the inside and totally unusable after the slightest damage."

2. *Nafir Suriyya* invokes Judgment Day directly twice: "Man's true homeland is not in this world but in the spiritual world beyond the grave. There he shall remain till the horn is sounded and he is resurrected for Judgment" (4, p. XX); "the Day of Judgment has arrived at our gates" (6, p. XX).

3. The native Protestant, John Wortabet, used the term *al-buq* for trumpet in the lecture "The Extent and Causes of the Proliferation of Science in Syria in this Generation": "If only I had a trumpet to let its sound shake up all of these lands for the rise of dawn to get up and work" (al-Bustani 1990e: 33).

4. Israfil "will blow the trumpet from a holy rock in Jerusalem to announce the Day of Resurrection. The trumpet is constantly poised at his lips, ready to be blown when God so orders. In Jewish and Christian biblical literature, Rafael is the counterpart of Israfil." www. britannica.com/EBchecked/topic/296909/Israfil.

5. "Sweet sound of the patriot's clarion would have been drowned out by the crude drumbeat of partisanship" (p. XX).

6. *Syria* was a term the ancient Greeks introduced. It was not used in the Bible. See Hitti 1951 for the early history of the term, and Rollinger 2006 for an etymological study of the conflation of ancient Assyria and Syria.

7. For example, in issue 10: "And whoever compares Syria's current ratio of harvests to population to that of ancient times will notice that its productivity, the wealth of its people, and its government can be increased manifold based on its natural resources."

8. Philipp 2004.

9. Smith 1833: 147.

10. Hanssen 2005a; Hill 2015a: 89–95, 2017. In his lecture on Arab culture in 1859, al-Bustani himself heaped praise on *Hadiqat al-Akhbar*'s "owner and beloved manager, Khalil Effendi al-Khuri. . . . He will be remembered forever among our compatriots as a conqueror of the most formidable fortress, of whose benefits previous generations were ignorant. Khalil al-Khuri stands at the shore of the great sea separating the Old World from the New World, peering out momentarily toward the New, then momentarily glancing back toward the Old. In his series of poems that marks the new age [later collected in *al-'Asr al-Jadid,* Beirut, 1863], al-Khuri pours classical poetry into a new mold." Adapted from S. Sheehi's translation in El-Ariss 2018: 8.

11. K. Khuri 1860, quoted in Zachs 2004: 33.

12. Makdisi 1997.

13. Sacks 2015: 83.

14. See Choueiri 2003: 39–67.

15. The rediscovery of "Queen Zenobia," who according to Choueiri (2003: 51, 57, 66) had become a popular didactic figure in the *Nahda,* is a case in point. Salim al-Bustani's morality tale "Zanubya malikat Tadmur," published in *al-Jinan* in the early 1870s, is based on Greco-Latin sources. Popularized by the French travel writer Baptistin Poujoulat, their heroic story of a tragic queen served the *Nahda*'s purpose better than the more sexually explicit and factionalist Arabic accounts of Zenobia. See Woltering 2014. By contrast, Tahtawi's representation of ancient Egypt appears to have worked the other way around: he complemented European Egyptology "with significant amounts of the Arabic textual tradition." Colla 2008: 122.

16. Kaufman 2011: 112.

17. *Wataniyya* would also take on anticolonial and progressive meanings in the post-war period. On this twentieth-century rivalry, see Havemann 2002; and Kaufman 2004.

18. For late-nineteenth- and twentieth-century uses and shifts in meaning of *wataniyya* and *qawmiyya,* see Rebhahn 1986; Peev 1987/1988; Bensaid 1987; Suleiman 2003.

19. *Muhit al-Muhit* (al-Bustani 1979: 129) defined *al-jinsiyya* in its identitarian sense as the condition of a kind, the constitution of belonging to or being from someplace.

20. It occupies a central position in the debate around gender in the Middle East, given that it has come to designate sex/sexuality in the 1930s. See Massad 2007 and Najmabadi 2013. As Peter Hill reminded us in a private communication, al-Bustani used the term *jins al-nisa'*—the female sex—in his preface to his *Robinson Crusoe* translation.

21. The *adib*—the writer—became consecrated as a distinct social figure in Egypt soon after *adab*-as-literature was institutionalized as an academic discipline. See Allan 2016.

22. This was a broader definition than that of his contemporary rival, Ahmad Faris al-Shidyaq, to whom the plural *al-adab* denoted literature and language studies only, not the hard sciences or the humanities more generally.

23. *Adab*-as-culture gradually came to be replaced by the twentieth-century neologism *al-thaqafa,* and Bustani was one of the first to introduce "the metaphorical use of *tathqif*" in *Muhit al-Muhit.* See Tibawi 1976.

24. Sachs offers this astute distinction: "If *Khutba fi adab al-ʿarab* privileges an understanding of the origin of language in relation to an originary, divine language, a language that is a ground, *asl,* and of which the Arabic, Syriac, and Hebrew languages are the temporal remnants, *Nafir Suriyya* privileges the body as a figure of unity in the interest of settling the past in the present" (Sacks 2015: 87). In *Muhit al-Muhit* (1869–70), too, *al-adab* retained "a relation to ethical comportment, it is 'a disposition that restrains one from carrying out what would disgrace him,' and its meaning includes 'to teach well-mannered and composed comportment and good morals *[al-akhlaq]*" (78).

25. al-Bustani 1990e: 64.
26. Arnold 1994: 8.
27. Mamdani 2004.
28. Hill 2015b: 117.

CHAPTER 5

1. Quoted in Duri 1987: 176n50. The last verse is repeated after each quatrain.
2. Lewis 1988: 41.
3. Quentin Skinner's (1982) critique of "the mythology of doctrines" governing the history of ideas is pertinent in this regard. Judging an author's (in)ability to anticipate concepts that only mattered later is shoddy scholarship. It includes the tendency to ascribe to a text ideas, intentions of a coherence that only later appeared, and the temptation to convert a given thinker's marginal remarks into a defining doctrine. Likewise, David Scott (1999: 5–9) insists that we need not only to historicize the answers a given text provides but also to "identify the question to which the proposition may be regarded as an answer."
4. For an early discussion, see Adib Ishaq, "al-Umma wa al-watan," republished in Sufayr 1904: 89–92. By contrast, Tahtawi used *milla, umma,* and *taʾifa* interchangeably in his *Takhlis* to translate all things national in France. The Tanzimat, in particular after the Crimean War, introduced the "millet system" and *milla* shrunk in meaning to denote particular non-Muslim communities in the empire; *umma* had grown to designate human multitudes that were, like the Muslim *umma,* not tied to a particular territory; *taʾifa* was the most loosely deployed

term of the three, generally used for a group of people within a whole, like a guild or sufi order, but it could also, as in his *Takhlis,* be used to designate the whole of the "French *ta'ifa* separated into royalists and liberals" in 1830. See Ayalon 1987: 19–28.

5. Koselleck 1989: 661.

6. For premodern occurrences and valances of *watan,* see Haarmann 2014; Antrim 2012; Noorani 2016; and Günther and Milich 2016.

7. Lewis 1991: 525–26.

8. Darling 2013; Boroujerdi 2013.

9. Khuri 1983: 22–23.

10. "*vatanın muhafazı için.*" *Mufassal* 1972: 2984. See also Abu-Manneh 1994.

11. al-Tahtawi included a history of the July Revolution in the final draft of his *Takhlis* at the behest of a French friend (Newman 2004: 84–85). According to Hourani (1983: 80–81), he translated the French revolutionary anthem. The Marseillaise's first line, "Allons enfants de la Patrie," may have echoed in *Nafir Suriyya*'s repeated dialogical invocations of *abna al-watan*—literally "the children of the homeland." Interestingly, Napoleon III (r. 1852–70) adopted "Partant pour la Syrie" as the Second French Empire's national anthem.

12. Newman (2004: 195–205). In an interesting slippage of the term that al-Tahtawi used for the revolution, *al-fitna* is rendered as *al-thawra* in R. Khuri's (1943: 180) original study; and as "civil war" in the English translation, R. Khuri (1983: 106).

13. For example, in *Takhlis,* Tahtawi translates "republican government" with *hukm al-jumhuriyya* and, for comparison, invokes the 1760s Hammam rebellion against the Mamluks in Upper Egypt as *jumhuriyya iltizamiyya.* See Newman (2004: 304). Conversely, Bustani invokes as a model of patriotic action the Antilyas Commune of 1840, whose leaders themselves invoked the French Revolution to stage a decisive uprising against the Egyptian occupation, in *Nafir Suriyya* 5 (November 1, 1860).

14. Tahtawi 1866, 1872–73.

15. Colla 2008: 121–36.

16. *Hubb al-watan min al-iman* was later emblazoned across the masthead of *al-Jinan.* It was the subject of an article in the journal's first year (*al-Jinan* [1870]: 302–3), reproduced in al-Bustani 1990i: 77–78.

It was also the slogan of the francophone Young Ottoman newspaper *Hürriyet*, published in Paris in the 1860s.

17. The status of this *hadith* is contested among scholars. The Baalbak-born Safavid polymath Baha al-Din al-ʿAmili (1547–1621) already argued against a nostalgic territorial interpetation of the *hadith* and against a bodily ascription to the concept of *watan*. Nevertheless, Iranian exiles in fin de siècle Istanbul rediscovered the power of this aphorism to express their homesickness. See Tavakoli-Targhi 1999: 115.

18. In the Islamic tradition, three principles have vied with one another over the meaning of *al-iman:* the Ashʿarite's insistence on internal conviction, the Hanafi-Maturidi stress on verbal expression, and others, including the Muʿtazilites, who prioritized the performative element of faith. Throughout Islamic history scholars were divided over questions of free will and faith, the existence of degrees of faith, if it can be partial, increase, and decrease. See Gardet 2012.

19. On *hubb al-watan* in *Nafir Suriyya,* see also Sheehi 2004: 57.

20. Makdisi 2008a.

21. Ahmad Faris al-Shidyaq, "Jumal adabiyya," republished in *majali al-ghurar li-kuttab al-qarn al-tasiʿ ʿashar* (Beirut, 1906), 189–91. Translated in Khuri 1983: 98–101.

22. *Nafir Suriyya* 4 (October 25, 1860).

23. *Nafir Suriyya* 6 (November 8, 1860). *al-Raʿiyya* is a key concept for Islamic governmentality. See Darling 2013. For an early critique of the concept, see Adib Ishaq, "al-malik wa al-raʿiyya," *Misr* (1877) republished in Sufayr 1904: 92–95.

24. Zolondek 1965; Ayalon 1987: 50–52.

25. *Nafir Suriyya* 4 (October 25, 1860).

26. Bou Ali 2013: 270.

27. ʿAmil 1986, Firro 2002, Weiss 2010.

28. "*Tawaʾif al-naml*," third issue; and "*tawaʾif al-hayawanat hatta . . . duda al-qazz*," eighth issue.

29. *al-gharadh* appears at least ten times (*al-aghradh* another seven times) in *Nafir Suriyya,* especially in the fifth issue ("Syria is . . . the birthplace of . . . this wicked carnal principle . . . inherited from barbarians . . . that has left behind destruction and peril and squandered the land's wealth and its families"); and in issues 9–11 (as the "selfish" antithesis of "the country's welfare," "true religion," and "noble guests

like morals and civilization"). In ʿAbbasid poetry, the *gharadh* section was the first part that conveyed the purpose of the subject of the poem. See Sajdi 2008: 186. For the linguists, *al-gharadh* is that for the sake of which the subject takes action and means *(ʿillat al-ghayya)*. In al-Bustani's *Muhit al-Muhit* (1979: 656), the first definitions of *al-gharadh* are about eating and drinking and suggest gluttony. In a derivative sense *al-gharad* also means "being loyal to one's faction." See also Saqr 2008: 21. El-Ariss (2013: 41) suggests that al-Tahtawi uses the term to express Mehmed Ali's Pasha's "desire" for military technology in his *Takhlis*.

30. *Nafir Suriyya* 3, 8, and 11.

31. Salim al-Bustani, "al-Gharadh," *al-Jinan* 18 (September 1870): 545–48.

32. Makdisi 2019.

CHAPTER 6

1. The Ottoman special envoy to the crisis, Fuʾad Pasha, had arrived in Beirut on August 8 and among his first acts was warning the Christians of Mount Lebanon "that it is not permissible for the subjects to take upon themselves the right of vengeance, as vengeance and punishment are the prerogatives of the government." See Makdisi 2000b: 147. A week later six thousand French soldiers led by General Charles Beaufort d'Hautpoul—erstwhile French chief of staff during Ibrahim Pasha's Syrian campaigns in the 1830s—disembarked "chanting the Crusaders song 'Partons pour la Syrie.'" Almost thirty thousand Christian refugees from Damascus and the Beqaa flocked to Beirut requiring urgent relief. In early September, Fuʾad Pasha issued dozens of summons on fugitive Druze leaders. The trial of the Ottoman governor of Saida, Hurshid Pasha, began September 17. On September 21, Saʿid Bey Jumblat and ten other Druze chiefs turned themselves in, only to be given the death sentence. A day before this first issue of *Nafir Suriyya,* the members of the International Commission of Inquiry were selected.

2. Militarily, the Druze warring factions of Mount Lebanon defeated their Maronite counterparts, whose religious leadership, most historians of Lebanon agree, incited the violence that ensued.

CHAPTER 7

1. Three days earlier, on October 5, the first session of the European Commission of Inquiry convened in Beirut. Maronite bishops started presenting lists of Druze perpetrators but the commission suspected that they "sought the political, as well as the physical, annihilation of their adversaries" (Farah 2000: 622).

2. For a full translation of the decree and Fu'ad Pasha's statements, see Abkarius 1920: 145–47.

3. Bustani refers to the biblical and Quranic (20:83) story of the Golden Calf: Impatient for the return of Moses from Mt. Sinai, the Israelites began to worship a golden calf. According to the Old Testament, Moses had three thousand male adults slain. A plague struck the tribe and God threatened to visit sin upon it: Exodus 19:20—32:11.

4. This phrase alludes to Quranic verse: *Sura al-Ra'd* 13:10–11.

CHAPTER 9

1. The ring/chain metaphor recurs in the ninth of *Nafir Suriyya,* where Bustani places Syria in the center of a global chain, which has become ever more connected since the rise of modern means of communication and transport.

2. The "right to life, honor, and prosperity" invokes the Ottoman Imperial Rescript of 1839.

3. This apocryphal *hadith,* popularized by Rifa'a al-Tahtawi in Egypt a generation earlier, was later to be the patriotic motto in al-Bustani's journal *al-Jinan* (1870–86). See chapter 5.

CHAPTER 10

1. al-Bustani used *qaba'il* in pamphlet 3 in relation to bees. Bee activity appears in the Quran (16:68) as cause for reflection. Ibn Khaldun's *Muqaddima* references the organization of bees to explain the royal authority system.

2. al-Bustani is referring to Ibrahim Pasha's Egyptian occupation of Bilad al-Sham from 1831 to 1840.

3. "Group of patriots" refers to the participants of the "Antilyas meeting"—a cross-confessional, anti-Egyptian uprising in the summer of 1840. For the proclamation text, see Rustum 1934: 102–3. See also Havemann 1983.

4. Qaysi-Yamani factionalism may have run through many parts of early modern Arab society but "it is only by the nineteenth century that this phenomenon starts being mentioned as the predecessor of the Yazbaki-Jumblati factionalism." See Abu Husayn 1991: 40. For more on these putative origins and permutations, see part 1 of this book.

5. See chapter 5 on the semantic shift of *al-jins* in Arabic.

6. The Matn was a confessionally mixed district of Mt. Lebanon at the time where violence broke out in 1841 and again in 1860.

CHAPTER 11

1. Or "to represent them adequately." *Tasawwaruha* also connotes "to represent." See Sacks 2015: 87.

2. The equivalent of around twenty-five million Ottoman piasters at the time.

3. The distinction between shepherds and flock represents the long-standing pastoral definition of the relationship between ruler and ruled in political advice literature. The Ottoman reforms challenged this form of governmentality.

CHAPTER 12

1. A list presented to the ninth session of the Commission on November 10, 1860, revealed that Fu'ad Pasha had expended over one and a half million piasters on the reconstruction of houses and allocated over two million piasters more toward the same end. See Farah 2000: 633–34. Many refugees started emigrating abroad via Beirut. On November 17, Yusuf Karam was provisionally appointed Christian *Qaimaqam* in Kisrawan. He was to lead the last anti-Ottoman rebellion in Mt. Lebanon from 1864 to 1866.

2. In other words, the loss of the homeland altogether is even graver then the loss of national harmony because the latter hardly existed before.

3. These are generic names often used in Arabic grammar books.

CHAPTER 13

1. In early December 1860, Lord Dufferin tabled a plan for a unified Syria. On December 12, General Beaufort provocatively marched his troops from Beirut to Saida. See Fawaz 1994: 125.

2. The Epistle to Titus is included in the New Testament. The author is thought to be St. Paul (5–67 AD), who wrote the letter at the end of his life. It instructs a fictitious Titus in the proper Christian conduct toward Cretan society and how to set up Christian missions there. On Bustani's solicitation of St. Paul, see Sacks 2015: 109–10. Bustani may do more than augment his scholarly credentials and reference a role-model Christian convert. In the context of discussing the Arabs confessing to lying, he also humors the play on deductive logic in the Cretan philosopher Epimenides's famous paradox: "All Cretans are liars."

3. Compare al-Bustani's point and his convoluted way of expressing it with James S. Mill's "II. Objection: That the People Are Not Capable of Acting Agreeably in Their Interest" in his *Essay on Government:* "One caution, first of all, we should take along with us, and it is this: that all those persons who hold the powers of government without having an identity of interests with the community, and all those persons who share in the profits which are made by the abuse of those powers, and all those persons whom the example and representations of the first two classes influence, will be sure to represent the community, or a part having an identity of interest with the community, as incapable in the highest degree of acting according to their own interest with the community ought to hold the power of government no longer, if those who have that identity of interest could be expected to act in any tolerable conformity with their interest" (Mill 1825: 29–30).

CHAPTER 14

1. On January 4, 1861, Fu'ad Pasha commenced the Mukhtara trial of seven hundred to eight hundred arrested Druzes. At the twentieth session, on January 24, the guilty lists were haggled over.

2. al-Bustani seems to have thought about his national school project as early as here. His *al-madrasa al-wataniyya* opened its doors two years later. See Hanssen 2005a.

3. Cf. Butrus al-Bustani, "Ta'lim al-nisa'" (1848).

CHAPTER 15

1. On February 7, the French position on death sentences softened. At the twenty-second session of the Commission on February 27, French consul Beclard agreed to pardon those condemned at Mukhtara but to execute "the Beirut Eleven." At the twenty-third session on February 28, Beclard consented to a stay of execution. Jumblat's guilt was discussed on March 2, the twenty-forth session, but he died of poor health on May 11, 1861, following seven months of incarceration.

2. Here, al-Bustani seems to be drawing on Ibn Khadun's stages of the rise and decline of dynasties.

3. On the Beirut-Damascus Road and other infrastructural developments, see Hanssen 2005b.

4. See Sheehi 2004: 57–61 for an elaboration on the metaphor of "the camel's hump."

CHAPTER 16

1. On March 16, the convicted Druzes were sent to exile in Tripoli (Libya).

2. al-Bustani invokes the historical sociology of Ibn Khaldun.

REFERENCES

BUTRUS AL-BUSTANI'S MAJOR PUBLICATIONS

al-Bustani, Butrus. 1843. *Kitab al bab al-maftuh fi a'mal al-ruh*. Translation of Eli Smith's notes on Protestant faith. Beirut.

———. c. 1844. *Siyahat masihi*. Translation of John Bunyan, *Pilgrim's Progress* (Beirut), originally published in 1678.

———. 1848a. *Kitab kashf al-Hijab fi 'ilm al-hisab*. Beirut.

———. c. 1848b. *Tarikh al-fida'*. Summary translation of Jean-Henri Merle d'Aubigné, *History of the Reformation* (Beirut), originally published in 1847.

———. 1851. *Rawdat al-tajir fi mask al-dafatir*. Beirut.

———. 1854. *Kitab misbah al-talib fi bahth al-matalib*. Beirut.

———. 1860a. *Diwan al-Mutanabbi*. Beirut.

———. 1860b. *Qissat As'ad Shidyaq bakura Suriyya*. Beirut.

———. 1861. *al-Tuhfa al-bustaniyya fi al-asfar al-kiruziyya*. Beirut: al-Maktaba al-Amirikiyya.

———. 1868a. *Miftah wa al-misbah (sarf wa nahw)*. Beirut.

———, ed. 1868b. *Tarikh Nabuliyun al-awal, imparatur faransi*. Beirut: Matba'a al-Wataniyya.

———. 1869. *Khitab fi al-hay'at al-ijtmi'iyya wa muqabalat bayna al-'awa'id al-'arabiya wa al-faranjiyya*. Beirut: Matba'a al-Ma'arif.

————. 1870. *Qutr al-Muhit*. Beirut: Matbaʿa al-Maʿarif.

————. 1876–1900. *Daʾirat al-Maʿarif*. Beirut: Matbaʿa al-Maʿarif.

————. 1979. *Muhit al-Muhit*. 2 vols. Beirut: Librairie du Liban. Originally published in 1869–70.

————. 1990a. "Amali falakiyya." In *al-Jamʿiyya al-Suriyya li al-ʿulum wa al-funun, 1847–1852*, edited by Y.Q. Khuri, 95–100. Beirut: Dar al-Hamra. Originally published in 1849.

————. 1990b. "Fi madina Bayrut." In *al-Jamʿiyya al-Suriyya li al-ʿulum wa al-funun, 1847–1852*, edited by Y.Q. Khuri, 71–72. Beirut: Dar al-Hamra. Originally published in 1849.

————. 1990c. "al-Hariri." In *al-Jamʿiyya al-Suriyya li al-ʿulum wa al-funun, 1847–1852*, edited by Y.Q. Khuri, 77–78. Beirut: Dar al-Hamra. Originally published in 1848.

————. 1990d. "Iktishaf jadid." In *al-Jamʿiyya al-Suriyya li al-ʿulum wa al-funun, 1847–1852*, edited by Y.Q. Khuri, 35. Beirut: Dar al-Hamra. Originally published in 1851.

————, ed. 1990e. *al-Jamʿiyya al-Suriyya li al-ʿulum wa al-funun, 1838–1852*. Edited by Y. Khuri. Beirut: Dar al-Hamra.

————. 1990f. "Khitab fi al-taʿlim al-nisaʾ." In *al-Jamʿiyya al-Suriyya li al-ʿulum wa al-funun, 1847–1852*, ed. by Y.Q. Khuri, 45–54. Beirut: Dar al-Hamra. Originally published in 1849.

————. 1990g. *Khutba fi al-adab al-ʿarab*. Beirut: al-Maktaba al-Amirikiyya. British Library 14555. c. 15. Reprinted in *al-Jamʿiyya al-Suriyya li al-ʿulum wa al-funun, 1847–1852*, edited by Y.Q. Khuri, 101–17. Beirut: Dar al-Hamra. Originally published in 1859.

————. 1990h. *Nafir Suriyya*. Beirut: Dar Fikr li al-Abhath wa al-Nashr. Originally published in 1860–61.

————. 1990i. *Nafir Suriyya*. Edited by Y. Khuri. Beirut: Dar al-Hamra.

————, ed. 1997. *Akhbar al-aʿyan fi Jabal Lubnan*, by Tannus Shidyaq, 2 vols. Beirut: Dar Lahad Khater. Originally published in 1959.

SECONDARY LITERATURE

Abkarius, Iskander Ibn Yaʿqub. 1920. *The Lebanon in Turmoil; Syria and the Powers in 1860: Book of the Marvels of the Time Concerning the Massacres in the Arab Country*. Translation and edited by J.F. Scheltema. New Haven: Yale University Press.

Abu Husayn, Abdul-Rahim. 1991. "The Feudal System of Mount Lebanon as Depicted by Nasif al-Yaziji." In *Quest for Understanding: Arabic and Islamic Studies in Honour of Malcolm H. Kerr,* edited by R. Baalbaki and P. Dodd, 33–42. Beirut: AUB Press.

Abu-Manneh, Butrus. 1980. "The Christians between Ottomanism and Syrian Nationalism: The Ideas of Butrus al-Bustani." *IJMES* 11:287–304.

———. 1994. "The Islamic Roots of the Gülhane Rescript." *Die Welt des Islam* 34:173–203.

Allan, Michael. 2016. *In the Shadow of World Literature: Sites of Reading in Colonial Egypt.* Princeton: Princeton University Press.

'Amil, Mahdi. 1986. *Fi al-dawla al-ta'ifiyya.* Beirut: Dar al-Farabi.

Antonius, George. 1939. *The Arab Awakening.* London: Hamilton.

Antrim, Zayde. 2012. *Routes and Realms: The Power of Place in the Early Islamic World.* Oxford: Oxford University Press.

El-Ariss, Tarek. 2013. *Trials of Arab Modernity: Literary Affects and the New Political.* New York: Fordham University Press.

———, ed. 2018. *The Arab Renaissance: A Bilingual Anthology of the* Nahda. New York: MLA Texts & Translations.

Armitage, David. 2012. "What's the Big Idea? Intellectual History and the *Longue Durée.*" *History of European Ideas* 38:493–507.

———. 2015. "Every Great Revolution Is a Civil War." In *Scripting Revolution: A Historical Approach to the Comparative Study of Revolutions,* edited by K. Baker and D. Edelstein, 57–68. Stanford: Stanford University Press.

Arnold, Mathew. 1994. *Culture and Anarchy.* New Haven: Yale University Press. Originally published in 1869.

Ayalon, Ami. 1987. *Language and Change in the Arab Middle East.* Oxford: Oxford University Press.

al-'Azm, Sadik Jalal. 1967/2011. *Self-Criticism after the Defeat.* Introduction by F. Ajami and a review by Ghassan Kanafani. London: Saqi Books.

Barbir, Karl. 1980. *Ottoman Rule in Damascus, 1708–1758.* Princeton: Princeton University Press.

Behrens Abouseif, Doris. 1992. "Gardens in Islamic Egypt." *Der Islam* 69:302–13.

Bensaid, Said. 1987. "*al-Watan* and *al-Umma* in Contemporary Arab Use." In *Foundations of the Arab State,* edited by G. Salamé, 149–74. New York: Routledge.

Beshara, Adel, ed. 2014. *Butrus al-Bustani. Spirit of the Age.* Melborne: Iphoenix.

Binay, Sarah, and Stefan Leder. 2012. *Translating the Bible into Arabic: Historical, Text-Critical and Literary Aspects.* Beirut: Orient Institute.

Bliss, Daniel. 1993. *Letters from a New Campus.* Edited by A. Howell. Beirut: AUB Press.

Booth, Marilyn. 2002. "'She Herself Was the Ultimate Rule': Arabic Biographies of Missionary Teachers and Their Pupils." *Islam and Christian-Muslim Relations* 13:433–38.

Boroujerdi, Mehrzad, ed. 2013. *Mirror for the Muslim Prince: Islam and the Theory of Statecraft.* Syracuse: Syracuse University Press.

Bou Ali, Nadia. 2012. "Collecting the Nation: Lexicography and National Pedagogy in *al-nahda al-ʿarabiyya.*" In *Archives, Museums and Collecting Practices in the Modern Arab World,* edited by S. Mejcher and J. Schwartz, 33–56. London: Ashgate.

———. 2013. "Butrus al-Bustani and the Shipwreck of the Nation." *Middle Eastern Literatures* 16:1–16.

Brockelmann, Carl. 1902. *Geschichte der Arabischen Literatur.* Vol. 2. Berlin: Emil Felber.

al-Bustani, Fuʾad Afram, ed. 1929. *al-Muʿallim Butrus al-Bustani.* Beirut.

al-Bustani, Salim. 1990. *Iftitahat Majalla al-Jinan al-Bayrutiyya, 1870–1884.* 2 vols. Edited by Y. Khuri. Beirut: Dar al-Hamra.

Carne, John. 1826. *Letters from the East.* Vol. 1. London.

Chevallier, Dominique. 1971. *La Société du Mont Liban à l'Epoche de la Révolution industrielle en Europe.* Paris: Librairie Orientaliste Paul Geuthner.

Choueiri Youssef. 2003. *Modern Arab Historiography: Historical Discourse and the Nation-State.* London: Routledge.

Colla, Elliott. 2003. "'Non, non! Si, si!': Commemorating the French Occupation of Egypt (1798–1801)." *MLN* 118:1043–69.

———. 2008. *Conflicted Antiquities Egyptology, Egyptomania, Egyptian Modernity.* Durham: Duke University Press.

Daghir, Sharbil. 2008. *al-ʿArabiyya wa al-tamaddun: Fi ishtibah al-ʿallaqa bayna al-nahda wa al-tamaddun.* Beirut: Dar al-Nahar.

Darling, Linda. 2013. *A History of Social Justice and Political Power in the Middle East: The Circle of Justice from Mesopotamia to Globalization.* London: Routledge.

Daya, Jean. 1981. *al-Mu'allim Butrus al-Bustani: Dirasat wa watha'iq.* Beirut: Majallat Fikr.

Dibs, Yusuf. 1893–1905. *Tarikh Suriyya.* 8 vols. Beirut.

Djaït, Hichem. 1989. *La Grande Discorde: Religion et politique dans l'Islam des origins.* Paris: Gallimard.

Duri, 'Abd al-'Aziz. 1987. *The Historical Formation of the Arab Nation: A Study in Identity and Consciousness.* Translation by L. I. Conrad. London: Croom Helm.

ElShakry, Marwa. 2013. *Reading Darwin in Arabic, 1860–1950.* Chicago: University of Chicago Press.

Farah, Caesar. 2000. *The Politics of Interventionism in Ottoman Lebanon, 1830–1861.* Oxford: Centre for Lebanese Studies, I. B. Tauris.

Fawaz, Leila. 1983. *Merchants and Migrants in Nineteenth-Century Beirut.* Cambridge, MA: Harvard University Press.

———. 1994. *An Occasion for War: Civil Conflict in Lebanon and Damascus in 1860.* London: I. B. Tauris and Centre for Lebanese Studies.

Firro, Kais. 2002. *Inventing Lebanon.* London: I. B. Tauris.

Gardet, L. 2012. "Īmān." In *Encyclopaedia of Islam,* 2nd ed., edited by P. Bearman, Th. Bianquis, C. E. Bosworth, E. van Donzel, W. P. Heinrichs, P. J. Bearman (vols. 10, 11, 12). Leiden: Brill.

Georgescu, Constantin I. 1978. *A Forgotten Pioneer of the Lebanese Nahdah: Salim al-Bustani, 1848–1884.* PhD diss., New York University.

Gilsenan, Michael. 1976. "Lying, Honor, and Contradiction." In *Transaction and Meaning: Directions in the Anthropology of Exchange and Symbolic Behavior,* edited by B. Kapferer, 191–219. Philadelphia: Institute for the Study of Human Issues.

Graf, Georg. 1949–51. *Geschichte der Christlichen Arabischen Literatur.* Vols. 3 and 4. Vatican City: Bibliotheka Apostolica.

Grafton, David. 2016. *The Contested Origins of the 1865 Arabic Bible.* Leiden: Brill.

Günther, Sebastian, and Stefan Milich, eds. 2016. *Representations and Visions of Homeland in Modern Arabic Literature.* Göttingen: OLMS Verlag.

Haarmann, Ulrich. 2002. "Mongols and Mamluk." In *Crisis and Memory in Islamic Societies,* edited by A. Pflitsch and A. Neuwirth, 165–76. Beirut: Orient Institute.

———. 2014. "Watan." In *Encyclopaedia of Islam,* 2nd ed., edited by P. Bearman, Th. Bianquis, C.E. Bosworth, E. van Donzel, and W.P. Heinrichs. Leiden: Brill.

Hakim, Carol. 2013. *The Origins of the Lebanese National Idea, 1840–1920.* Berkeley: University of California Press.

Hallaq, Boutros. 2014. "Adab E) Modern Usage." In *Encyclopaedia of Islam,* edited by K. Fleet, G. Krämer, D. Matringe, J. Nawas, and E. Rowson. Leiden: Brill.

Hamadeh, Shirine. 2008. *The City's Pleasures: Istanbul in the Eighteenth Century.* Seattle: University of Washington Press.

Hanssen, Jens. 2005a. "The Birth of an Education Quarter: Zokak el-Blat as a Cradle of Arabic Cultural Revival." In *History, Space and Social Conflict in Beirut: The Quarter of Zokak el-Blat,* edited by Ralph Bodenstein et al., 143–74. Beirut: German Orient Institute.

———. 2005b. *Fin de Siècle Beirut: The Making of an Ottoman Provincial Capital.* Oxford: Clarendon.

Hanssen, Jens, and Max Weiss. 2016. *Arabic Thought beyond the Liberal Age: Towards an Intellectual History of the Nahda.* New York: Cambridge University Press.

Havemann, Axel. 1983. *Rurale Bewegungen im Libanongebirge des 19. Jahrhunderts.* Berlin: Klaus Schwarz.

———. 2002. *Geschichte und Geschichtsverständnis im Libanon des 19. und 20. Jahrhunderts: Formen und Funktionen des historischen Selbstverständnisses.* Beirut: Orient Institute.

Hayek, Ghenwa. 2013. "Experimental Fictions; or, The Brief and Wonderous Life of the Nahda Sensation Story." *Middle Eastern Literatures* 16:249–65.

Hill, Peter. 2015a. "Early Arabic Translations of English Fiction: The Pilgrim's Progress and Robinson Crusoe." *Journal of Semitic Studies* 60 (1): 177–212.

———. 2015b. "Utopia and Civilization in the Arab Nahda." DPhil Thesis, Oxford.

———. 2017. "Arguing with Europe: Eastern Civilization versus Orientalist Exoticism." *PMLA* 123 (2): 405–12.

Hirschman, Albert O. 1977. *The Passions and the Interests: Political Arguments for Capitalism before Its Triumph.* Princeton: Princeton University Press.

Hitti, Philip. 1951. *History of Syria: Including Lebanon and Palestine.* London: MacMillan.

Holt, Elizabeth. 2009. "Narrative and Reading Public in 1870s's Beirut." *Journal of Arabic Literature* 40:37–70.

———. 2014. "From Gardens of Knowledge to Ezbekiyya after Midnight: The Novel and the Arabic Press from Beirut to Cairo, 1870–1892." *Middle Eastern Literatures* 16:232–48.

———. 2017. *Fictitious Capital: Silk, Cotton, and the Rise of the Arabic Novel.* New York: Fordham University Press.

Horne, Alistair. 1977. *A Savage War for Peace: Algeria, 1954–1962.* New York: Viking.

Hourani, Albert. 1983. *Arabic Thought in the Liberal Age.* Cambridge: Cambridge University Press. Originally published in 1962.

———. 1990. "Bustani's Encyclopaedia." *Journal of Islamic Studies* 1:111–19.

Hurewitz, J.C. 1975. *The Middle East and North Africa in World Politics.* New Haven: Yale University Press.

Inalcik, Halil. 1973. "Application of the Tanzimat and Its Social Effects." *Archivum Ottomanicum* 5:97–127.

Issa, Rana. 2017. "The Arabic Language and Syro-Lebanese National Identity: Searching in Butrus al-Bustani's Muhit al-Muhit." *Journal of Semitic Studies:* 465–84.

al-Jabarti, ʿAbd al-Rahman. 1993. *Napoleon in Egypt: al-Jabarti's Chronicle of the French Occupation of Egypt in 1798.* Translated by S. Moreh. Princeton: Wiener.

Jandora, John W. 1981. "Butrus al-Bustani: Ideas, Endeavours, and Influence." PhD diss., University of Chicago.

Jeha, Shafik. 2004. *Darwin and the Crisis of 1882 in the Medical Department.* Translated by S. Kaya. Beirut: AUB Press.

Jessup, Henry. 1910. *Fifty-Three Years in Syria.* Vol. 2. New York: Fleming Revell.

Kaufman, Asher. 2004. *Reviving Phoenicia: The Search for an Identity in Lebanon.* London: I.B. Tauris.

———. 2011. "Henri Lammens and Syrian Nationalism." In *Origins of Syrian Nationhood: Histories, Pioneers and Identities,* 108–22. London: Routledge.

Kesrouany, Maya. 2015. "Stranded in Arabic: *Robinson Crusoe* in Beirut." *Comparative Literary Studies* 52 (2): 289–317.

Khalidi, Rashid. 2004. *Resurrecting Empire: Western Footprints and American's Perilous Path in the Middle East.* Boston: Beacon.

Khalidi, Rashid, Lisa Anderson, et al., eds. 1991. *The Origins of Arab Nationalism.* New York: Columbia University Press.

Khalidi, Tarif. 2002. "The Battle of the Camel: Trauma, Memory and Reconciliation." In *Crisis and Memory in Islamic Societies,* edited by A. Pflitsch and A. Neuwirth, 153–64. Beirut: Orient Institute.

Khater, Akram Fouad. 2001. *Inventing Home: Emigration, Gender, and the Middle Class in Lebanon, 1870–1920.* Berkeley: University of California Press.

Khuri, Khalil. 1860. *Kharabat Suriyya.* Beirut: Matbaʿa Suriyya.

Khuri, Raʾif. 1943. *al-Fikr al-ʿarabi al-hadith: Athar al-thawra al-firansiyya fi tawjihi al-siyasi wa al-ijtimaʿi.* Beirut: Matabiʿ al-Kashshaf.

———. 1983. *Modern Arab Thought: Channels of the French Revolution to the Arab East.* Translated by I. ʿAbbas. Revised and edited by C. Issawi. Princeton: Kingston.

Khuri, Yusuf Q. 1995. *al-Rajul sabiq li-ʿasrihi: al-Muʿallim Butrus Bustani, 1819–1883.* Beirut: Bisam.

Kornbluh, Anna. 2013. *Realizing Capital: Financial and Psychic Economies in Victorian Form.* New York: Fordham University Press.

Koselleck, Reinhart. 1989. "Linguistic Change and the History of Events." *Journal of Modern History* 61:649–66.

Krämer, Gudrun. 2006. *Geschichte Palästinas.* Munich: Becksche Reihe.

Labaki, Butrus. 1984. *Introduction à l'histoire economic du Liban: Soie et commerce extérieur en fin de periode ottoman, 1840–1914.* Beirut: Publications de Université Libaanaise.

Lewis, Bernard. 1988. *The Political Language of Islam.* Chicago: University of Chicago Press.

———. 1991. "Watan." *Journal of Contemporary History* 26:523–33.

Lindner, Christine B. 2014. "Rahil ʿAta al-Bustani: Wife and Mother of the Nahda." In *Butrus al-Bustani: Spirit of the Age,* edited by A. Beshara. Melborne: IPhoenix.

Makdisi, Ussama. 1997. "Reclaiming the Land of the Bible: Missionaries, Secularism, and Evangelical Modernity." *AHR* 102:680–713.

———. 2000a. "Corrupting the Sublime Sultanate: The Revolt of Tanyus Shahin in Nineteenth-Century Ottoman Lebanon." *Comparative Studies in Society and History* 42:180–207.

————. 2000b. *Culture of Sectarianism: Community, History and Violence in Nineteenth Century Ottoman Lebanon*. Berkeley: University of California Press.

————. 2002. "Ottoman Orientalism." *American Historical Review* 107:768–96.

————. 2004. "After 1860: Debating Religion, Reform, and Nationalism in the Ottoman Empire." *IJMES* 34:601–17.

————. 2008a. *Artillery of Heaven: American Missionaries and the Failed Conversion of the Middle East*. Ithaca: Cornell University Press.

————. 2008b. "Moving beyond Orientalist Fantasy, Sectarian Polemic, and Nationalist Denial." *IJMES* 40:599–60.

————. 2015. "Diminished Sovereignty and the Impossibility of 'Civil War' in the Middle East." *American Historical Review* 120:1739–52.

————. 2019. *The Ecumenical Frame: Coexistence and Sectarianism in the Middle East*. Berkeley: University of California Press.

Mamdani, Mahmood. 2004. *Good Muslim, Bad Muslim: America, the Cold War and the Roots of Terror*. New York: Three Leaves Press & Doubleday.

Marx, Karl. 1968. "Disturbances in Syria." *New York Daily Tribune*, August 11, 1860 [filed from London, July 28, 1860]. Republished in *Karl Marx on Colonialism and Modernization,* edited by S. Avineri, 398–400. New York: Doubleday.

Massad, Joseph. 2007. *Desiring Arabs*. Chicago: Chicago University Press.

Matar, Elias. 1874. *al-ʿUqud al-durriyya fi tarikh al-mamlaka Suriyya*. Beirut.

McCarthy, Justin. 2015. *Turks and Armenians: Nationalism and Conflict in the Ottoman Empire*. Madison WI: Turko-Tatar Press.

Mill, James S. 1825. *Essays on Government*. London: Innes.

Mishaqa, Mikhaʾil. 1988. *Murder, Mayhem, and Pillage: The History of the Lebanon in the 18th and 19th Centuries*. Translated and edited by Wheeler M. Thackston. Albany: State University of New York Press.

Mitchell, Timothy. 1988. *Colonizing Egypt*. Cambridge: Cambridge University Press.

Mufassal Osmanlı tarihi, resimli-haritalı. 1972. Vol. 6. Istanbul: Güven Basimevi.

Najmabadi, Afsaneh. 2013. "The Genus of Sex or the Sexing of *Jins*." *IJMES* 45:211–25.

Newman, Daniel. 2004. *An Imam in Paris: al-Tahtawi's Visit to France, 1826–1831.* London: Saqi.

Noorani, Yaseen. 2016. "Estrangement and Selfhood in the Classical Concept of *Watan.*" *Journal of Arabic Literature* 47:16–42.

Peev, Yordan. 1987/1988. "Developpement et particularités de d'idée de la 'nation arabe' (2ème moitié du XIX-début du XXe siècle)." *Quaderni di Studi Arabi* 5/6:616–27.

Philipp, Thomas. 2002. *Acre: The Rise and Fall of a Palestinian City—World-Economy and Local Politics.* New York: Columbia University Press.

———. 2004. "Identities and Loyalties in Bilad al-Sham at the Beginning of the Early Modern Period." In *From the Syrian Land to the States of Syria and Lebanon,* edited by T. Philipp and C. Schumann, 9–26. Beirut: Orient Institute.

al-Qays, Faiz 'Alam al-Din. 2005. *Athar al-mu'allim Butrus al-Bustani fi al-nahda al-wataniyya fi Lubnan.* Beirut: Dar al-Farabi.

Rebhan, Helga. 1986. *Geschichte und Funktion einiger politischer Termini im Arabischen des 19. Jahrhunderts.* Wiesbaden: Harrassowitz.

Reinaud, M. 1858. *Notice sur la gazette arabe de Beyrout, lue dans la séance génerale de la Société Asiatique du 29 Juin 1858.* Paris: Imprimerie Impériale.

Rodogno, Davide. 2012. *Against Massacre: Humanitarian Interventions in the Ottoman Empire, 1815–1914.* Princeton: Princeton University Press.

Rollinger, Robert. 2006. "'Assyria' and 'Syria' Again." *Journal of Near Eastern Studies* 65:283–87.

Rustum, Asad. 1934. *Usul 'arabiyya li-tarikh Suriyya/Materials for a Corpus of Arabic documents.* Vol. 5.

———. 1956–57. *Bashir bayna al-Sultan wa-al-'Aziz: 1804–1841.* Beirut: Manshurat al-Jami'at al-Lubnaniya.

Sacks, Jeffrey. 2007. "Futures of Literature: *Inhitat, Adab, Naqd.*" *Diacritics* 37:32–55.

———. 2015. *Iterations of Loss: Mutilation and Aesthetic Form, al-Shidyaq to Darwish.* New York: Fordham University Press.

Sajdi, Dana. 2008. "Revisiting Layla Akhyaliya's Trespass." In *Transforming Loss into Beauty: Essays on Arabic Literature and Culture in Honor of Magda al-Nowaihi,* edited by M. Hammond and D. Sajdi, 185–227. Cairo: AUC Press.

Salibi, Kamal. 1988. *A House of Many Mansions: The History of Lebanon Reconsidered.* Berkeley: University of California Press.

Saqr, Yusuf Saqr. 2008. *'A'ilat Hakamat Lubnan.* Beirut: al-Markaz al-'Arabi lil-Ma'lumat.

Sarmiento, Domingo. 2004. *Facundo: Civilization and Barbarism.* Berkeley: University of California Press. Originally published in 1845.

Sawaya, Mikha'il. 1963. *al-Mu'allim Butrus al-Bustani, Dirasa.* Beirut: Matabi' al-Karim.

Scott, David. 1999. *Refashioning Futures: Criticism after Postcoloniality.* Princeton: Princeton University Press.

Sharabi, Hisham. 1970. *Arab Intellectuals and the West: The Formative Year, 1875–1914.* Baltimore: Johns Hopkins University Press.

Sheehi, Stephen. 1997. "Epistemography of the Modern Arab Subject: al-Mu'allim Butrus al-Bustani's *Khutbah Fi Adab-al-'Arab.*" *Public* 16: *Entangled Territories:* 65–84.

———. 2000. "Inscribing the Arab Self: Butrus al-Bustani and the Paradigms of Subjective Reform." *British Journal of Middle Eastern Studies* 27:7–24.

———. 2004. *Foundations of Modern Arab Identity.* Gainesville: University Press of Florida.

———. 2012. "Towards a Critical Theory of *al-Nahdah:* Epistemology, Ideology and Capital." *Journal of Arabic Literature* 43:269–98.

———. 2016. *The Arab Imago.* Princeton: Princeton University Press.

Skinner, Quentin. 1988. "Meaning and Understanding in the History of Ideas." In *Meaning and Context, Quentin Skinner and His Critics,* edited by J. Tully, 29–68. London: Polity.

Smith, Eli. 1833. *Missionary Sermons and Addresses.* Boston.

Steppat, Fritz. 1972. "Eine Bewegung unter den Notablen Syriens." In *XVII Deutscher Orientalistentag vom 21.–27. 1968 in Würzburg,* edited by W. Voigt.

Sufayr, Yusuf. 1904. *Majali al-ghurar li-kuttab al-qarn al-tasi' 'ashar.* Vol. 1, pt. 1. Cairo: Maktaba al-Madaris.

Suleiman, Yasir. 2003. *The Arabic Language and National Identity.* Edinburgh: Edinburgh University Press.

al-Suwaidi, 'Abd al-Rahman. 2003. *Tarikh Baghdad aw hadiqat al-zawra'*. Edited by 'I. 'Abd al-Salam Ra'uf. Baghdad: Dar al-Hikma.

Suwaya, Mikha'il. 1963. *al-Mu'allim Butrus al-Bustani*. Beirut: Maktabat al-Bustani.

Tageldin, Shaden. 2011. *Disarming Words: Empire and the Seduction of Translation in Egypt*. Los Angeles: University of California Press.

al-Tahtawi, Rif'at al-Rifa'i. 1866. *Kitab al-manahij al-albab al-misriyya fi manahij al-adab al-'asriyya*. Bulaq: al-Matba'a al-Kubra al-Amiriyya.

———. 1872–73. *al-Murshid al-amin li al-banat wa al-banin*. Cairo: Matba'at al-Madaris al-Malakiyya.

Tarazi, Philippe de. 1913. *Tarikh al-sahafa al-'arabiyya*. Vol. 1. Beirut: Matba'a al-Adabiyya.

Tavakoli-Targhi, Mohamad. 1999. *Refashioning Iran: Orientalism, Occidentalism and Historiography*. London: Palgrave MacMillan.

Tibawi, Abdulatif. 1963. "The American Missionaries in Beirut and Butrus al-Bustani." *St. Antony's Papers* 16:137–82.

———. 1976. "The Meaning of ath-Thaqafa in Contemporary Arabic." In *Arabic and Islamic Themes; Historical, Educational and Literary Studies*, 286–92. London: Luzac.

Traboulsi, Fawwaz. 2007. *A History of Modern Lebanon*. London: Pluto Press.

al-Ustawani, Muhammad Sa'id. 1994. *Mashahid wa-ahdath Dimashqiya fi muntasaf al-qarn al-tasi' 'ashar*. Damascus.

Weiss, Max. 2010. *In the Shadow of Sectarianism: Law, Shi'ism, and the Making of Modern Lebanon*. Cambridge MA: Harvard University Press.

Winter, Stefan. 2010. *The Shiites of Lebanon under Ottoman Rule*. Cambridge: Cambridge University Press.

Woltering, Robbert. 2014. "Zenobia or al-Zabba: The Modern Arab Literary Reception of the Palmyran Protagonist." *Middle Eastern Literatures* 17:25–42.

Yanni, Jurji. 1881. *Tarikh Suriyya*. Beirut.

al-Yaziji, Nasif. 2002. *Risala tarikhiyya fi ahwal Jabal Lubnan al-iqta'i*. Edited by Muhammad Khalil al-Basha and Riyyad Husayn Ghannam. Beirut: Dar Ma'an.

Zachs, Fruma. 2001. "Toward a Proto-Nationalist Concept of Syria: Revisiting the American Presbyterian Missionaries in the Nineteenth-Century Levant." *Die Welt des Islams:* 145–73.

————. 2004. "Building a Cultural Identity: The Case of Khalil Khuri." In *From the Syrian Land to the States of Syria and Lebanon,* edited by T. Philipp and C. Schumann, 27–39. Beirut: Orient Institute.

————. 2005. *The Making of a Syrian Identity; Intellectuals and Merchants in Nineteenth Century Beirut.* Leiden: Brill.

————. 2011. "Subversive Voices of Daughters of the *Nahda:* Alice al-Bustani and *Riwayat Saʾiba* (1891)." *Hawwa* 9:332–57.

Zolondek, Leon. 1965. "*Ash-Shaʿb* in Arabic Political Literature in the 19th Century." *Die Welt des Islams* 10:1–16.

Zurayk, Constantine. 1948/1956. *The Meaning of Disaster.* Beirut: Khayat's.

INDEX

ʿAbd al-Qadir al-Qabbani, 24
Abdülhamid II, Sultan, 7–8, 36
Abdülmecid I (ʿAbd al-Majid),
  Sultan, 68, 135n27
abnaʾ al-watan (compatriots), 22, 42,
  52, 56, 58
Abu-Manneh, Butrus, 38
al-adab/adabi (morals/education):
  See also civil war of 1860 moral
  losses and moral gains; culture,
  108, 123, 129, 144n29; morals,
  81, 103, 121, 124, 141n24; translation of, 50, 50–51, 140n21-23,
  140nn21-23, 141n24
ādāb al-ʿArab ("The Culture of the
  Arabs"), 50
affective registers, 22, 24, 41, 58
Akhbar al-aʿyan fi Jabal Lubnan, 14
al-akhlaq (morals). See *al-adab/adabi*
al-nafir meaning, 45
ambivalence of introspection, 4
American mission/% and
  al-Bustani in Beirut, 25–27;
  al-Bustani's break with, 28–29;

"liberal caucus" of, 30; and
  Nahda national and scientific
  outlooks, 8; and the "native
  academy," 30; and Protestant
  notions of cultural superiority,
  40; and racial stereotypes, 50;
  and Shidyaq's abduction and
  death, 27–28, 135n25; and Syria
  as patriotic ideal, 47
American Mission School for
  Girls, 26
Antilyas meeting, 18, 82, 142n13,
  146n3
anti-sectarianism, xiii–xiv, 2,
  59–62
Antonius, George, 26, 35, 37, 136n3
Arabic culture, "pure," 33–34
Arabic encyclopaedia, (*Daʾirat
  al-Maʿarif—al-Jinan*), 33, 136n42
Arabic language: as cultural unifier,
  29, 36, 120; revival, revision and
  innovation of, 8–9, 29
Arabic lexicon, *Muhit al-Muhit*,
  33–34

Arabic serial novel, 43

Arab intellectual history, 3–4

Arab nationalism: *See also hubb al-watan; al-watan*; al-Bustani's civilizing project, 41; diachronic post-Ottoman schemas, 48, 140n17; as ecumenical, 53–54; foundational trope of crisis, 42; and love of the homeland (Syria), 36, 39, 41, 54, 76–78; and Phoenicianism, 48–49; and political belonging and attachment, 49, 53

Arnold, Matthew, 7, 51

ʿAta, Rahil (wife), 26, 135n20

al-ʿAttar, Hasan, 3

"Awake ye Arabs Awake,," 43, 138n30

al-awtan. See *al-watan*

ʿAyn Warqa boarding school, 24, 25

al-ʿAzm, Sadik, 4

al-Bab al-maftuh fi ʿamal al-ruh, 25

Babel of religions, 36, 57, 120

Bab Tuma massacre (Damascus), 4, 39

Barr al-Sham. *See* Bilad al-Sham

Bashir II al-Shihabi, emir, 15–17

battle of petitions, 18–19

Battle of the Camel, 3, 6

Bayhum, Husayn, 24, 32

Beaufort d'Hautpoul, Charles de (General), 21, 133n23, 144n1

bees, 59–60, 73, 145n1c

"Beirut School," 138n25

Bérad, Victor, 48

Berlant, Lauren, 58–59

Bible translation, 9, 27, 28, 135n19

Bilad al-Sham: *See also* economic development; Arabic as cultural unifier in, 29, 36, 120; British and Ottoman opponents of communal segregation, 21–22; and Egyptian occupation and centralization, 17–18, 81, 145n2c; establishment and administrative system, 15; integration with coastal and mountain regions, 14; political semantics of "Syria" designation, 46–47; relative autonomy of Shihabi rule in, 14; as territory for a "Syrian Nation," 22, 38–39; as *al-watan*, 76

Bishop of Saida, 21

Bliss, Daniel, 31, 47

Bolívar, Simón, 74

Bou Ali, Nadia, 42, 58

Britain, 5, 18

al-Bustani, Najib (son), 8

al-Bustani, Abdallah (nemesis-uncle), 21, 22

al-Bustani, Butrus, —biography: overview, 7–10; family and early life, 23; early education and move to Beirut, 24; Protestantism, 25–26, 27, 40; marriage, 26, 135n20

al-Bustani, Butrus, —politics: ecumenical liberal pluralism of, 28, 36, 95–96; as loyal Ottoman subject, 36, 68, 115; Ottomanism of, 38; on Shidyaq's death, 28; support for Fuʾad Pasha's pacification, 37, 68, 94

al-Bustani, Butrus, —significance of: conceptualization of racism before the word, 50; key figure in *Nahda*, 23; linguistic and cultural revival, 29, 43–44; modern Lebanese reclamation of, 38; presaged failure of sectarian political system in Lebanon, 39

al-Bustani, Butrus, —subjectivity: affective registers in his

works, 22, 24, 41, 58; bourgeois
sensibilities, 2, 41, 42; challenged
Christian sectarianism/racism,
40; and civil war, 6; conflicting
loyalties, 37; as internal exile,
24–25, 59; as liberal, 41–42;
unencumbered with colonial/
nationalist geography of nations,
49; urban bias of, 51, 122–23
al-Bustani, Butrus, —works: after
Nafir Suriyya, 29–34; civil war
neologism (*al-harb al-ahliyya*),
6; English Arabic translations,
25, 27; as lexicographer, 30,
33–34; *Nafir Suriyya* authorship,
6–7; Orientalist adoption of
racist taxonomy, 51; salons, 27,
135n21; as teacher, lecturer and
dragoman, 27; three important
reform texts, 41; translation and
interpretation, 8–9, 27
al-Bustani, Salim (son), 7, 30, 59, 61,
134n13, 140n15

capitalism and culture, 42–43,
138n25
Christians. *See* American mission/
missionaries; Maronites;
Protestantism
civilization (*al-tamaddun*): Arabic,
34, 52; barbarity as antithesis of,
65, 82, 97, 103, 123; and concord,
41, 58, 77–78, 129; as cultivation
of the self and virtue, 123–25; as
emancipatory, 36; European, 125,
127; fake, 123–24, 126; fanaticism
as antithetical to, 2, 106–7, 115–16;
and governance, 128–29; (true) as
individual and collective development, 51; and true religion,
60, 128; as urban modernity, 32,
51, 122–23; Western, 2–5, 125, 127;
and work-ethic, 42, 51, 104

civil war: euphemisms/alternative
terms for, 6, 132n18; in Middle
East, 3; as Roman invention,
132n19
civil war of 1860, —causes: capitalist penetration, 41–42; Christian
attacks on Druze villages, 20,
144n2; class conflict, 14; *dual
qaimaqamate,* 19–20; European
intervention, 21–22, 29; European-
Ottoman rivalries, 16–17; in
historiography,, 13–14; Jumblat-
Yazbaki/Qaysi-Yamani factionalism, 22, 82, 146n4; outbreak,
20; prejudice, 60; rivalries
between notables, 15–17, 110–11;
social unrest and Egyptian
occupation, 17–18
civil war of 1860, —consequences: Dayr al-Qamar and
Damascus massacres, 20, 39;
death toll and material losses,
29, 85–86, 146n1b; European
intervention, 21–22, 29; impact
on all of "Syria," 22; impact on
al-Bustani's family, 26; Ottoman
pacification, 21, 37, 40, 148n1; refugees, 29, 68–69, 144n1; repres-
sion of leaders, 144n1, 148n1
civil war of 1860, —costs:
accounting of material losses,
37, 85–89; charity and state
aid, 89–90, 146n2b; of house
reconstructions, 146n1c
civil war of 1860, —moral gains:
ability to take responsibility,
110; awareness of horrors of war,
106; awareness of the need for
good governance and laws, 111;
charity, 89–90; connection with
the world, 109–10; rulers' awareness of need for security and
competent leadership, 115

civil war of 1860, —moral losses: the corruption of manners and morals, 103; failure to punish perpetrators, 93–94; lessons learned, 95–96; loss of concord, 94–95; loss of family honor, 103; loss of material comfort, 101–2; loss of self-respect, 98–99; loss of trust, 102–3

civil war, —prevention of: concord, 106–7, 113; equal access to education, 108; material security and well-being, 119; meritocracy in government appointments, 108, 116; separation of religious and political authority, 2, 36, 38, 96, 107, 117–18

The Clarion of Syria. See *Nafir Suriyya*

clarion (patriotic) vs. drum (prejudiced), 2, 84, 123, 138n1, 139n5

"clever personality" syndrome (*al-fahlawiyyah*), 4

community of suffering, 47

compatriots (*abna' al-watan*): "countrymen," 22, 56, 58, 42 52; responsible thinkers '*uqala'* vs. hoodlums (*awbash*), 58; as synthesis of Arab/European elements, 52; and Syria as affective community, 22

compensation for losses, 68–70, 145n3

concord: and civilization, 41, 58, 77–78, 129; fanaticism as the antithesis of, 36; necessity of for the homeland, 94; and prevention of civil war, 35–36, 113

Crimean War, 5

Crusader sacking of Jerusalem, 3, 131n6

cultural atavism, vs. work-ethic for al-Bustani, 42

Culture and Anarchy (1867), 7

Da'irat al-Ma'arif—al-Jinan (Arabic encyclopaedia), 33, 136n42

Darwin, Charles, 8

Day of Resurrection. *See* Day of Judgment

Dayr al-Qamar, crisis and massacre, 19–20

Declaration of the Rights of Man and Citizen of 1789, 55

Defoe, Daniel, 9, 42

dhamma (to bring close/associate with), 137n15

Dibs, Yusuf, 47

Diwan, 9

doctrine of justification by faith, 25

domestic love, 26, 134n13

"double consciousness," 41

doubt, 37, 137n4

drum (prejudiced) vs. clarion (patriotic), 84, 123, 138n1, 139n5

the Druze: Fakhr al-Din II al-Ma'ani, 13, 15, 19; the Jumblats, 16, 21, 82, 146n4, 148n1; as landlords over Maronite peasants, 17, 23; Ottoman and British backing of, 5, 18–19; Ottoman pursuit of fugitive leaders, 144n1; Ottoman reorganization of after Egyptian occupation, 18–19; trials and punishment of, 148n1, 1b, 1c

Druze-Maronite narrative: and al-Yaziji-Shidyaq's "feudal order" interpretation, 22; religious rivalry argument, 13–14

dual qaimaqamate, 19–20

Dufferin, Lord, 21–22, 147n1

al-Duwayhi, Istifan, 13

Dyck, Cornelius Van, 25, 27, 30

economic development: cultural production (Beirut), 32–33, 138n25; European merchant capital, 17; railways and communication, 120, 145n1b; silk trade, 17, 23, 33, 42–43

ecumenical religiosity: guaranteed by love of the homeland, 57; and reliance on nation form, 54

education (*al-ta'lim*), 50; Arabic as language of instruction, 120; for commoners, 0; for politically and socially responsible subjects, 30; for women, 108

Egypt, French invasion of, 3

Egyptian occupation: and Antilyas meeting, 18, 82, 142n13, 146n3; commoner revolts against, 17–18; and Ibrahim Pasha, 15, 144n1; Syria as caught between Egypt and Ottomans, 81, 145n2c

Epistle to Titus, 101, 147n2b

equality: and al-Bustani's pro-Ottoman position, 28; and diversity, xiv; and hybrid identity and coexistence, 40; as language of Maronite challenge to Druze authority, 19; and religious freedom, 36

European imperialism. *See* Western imperialism

European intervention: al-Bustani's support for, 65–66, 111–12; duplicity and opportunism of, 4–5; and Egyptian occupation, 17–18; and the "Franco-Lebanese dream," 21–22, 133n26

European-Ottoman rivalry, impact on Mount Lebanon social order, 16

factionalism (*tahazzubat*), 60; apply punishment without revenge, 65–66; Jumblat-Yazbaki/Qaysi-Yamani, 22, 82, 146n4; Maronites vs. emirs, 16, 65; as negation of justice, 61, 80, 112

Facundo (1845), 7

al-fahlawiyyah ("clever personality" syndrome), 4

faith, *al-watan* as an element of, 53, 56, 77

Fakhr al-Din II al-Ma'ani (Druze), 13, 15, 19

false patriot, 57–58

fanaticism (ta'assub): as antithetical to civilization and progress, 2, 106–7, 115–16; and al-Bustani's modern resonance, xiv, 35; and *hubb* (love), 57; and Muslim stereotyping, 39; vs. mutual respect between faiths and concord, 36; and two types of religiosity, 41, 58, 77–78; and underlying prejudice, 60, 107

"feudal order" consensus narrative, 14, 20, 22

"Fi al-ta'lim al-nisa'," 50

Fichte, Johann Gottlieb, 7

al-fitna (discord), 6

foreign invasions in Middle Eastern history, 3

France: and dream of Christian sovereignty, 21–22, 133n26; and geographic determinism, 47–48; Maronite project, 18; motives behind humanitarian intervention, 5; "Franco-Lebanese dream," 21–22, 133n26

freedom of conscience, 40, 56, 77, 118

French Constitutional Charter, 55

French revolutions, al-Tahtawi
and al-Bustani inspired by, 55,
142nn11,13
Fuʾad Pasha: his Ottomanism
assessed against al-Bustani's,
40; inadmissibility of "right of
vengeance," 144n1; opposition
to communal segregation and
"Franco-Lebanese dream," 21,
22; pacification mission, 21, 37,
40, 68
"future's past," 40

gardens metaphor, 32–33
gender and *al-jins* concept, 140n20
geographical determinism and
Syria, 46–48
geographical imagination, 47,
53–54
German unification, 5
al-gharadh (prejudice): *See also* sectarianism; antithesis of patriotism, 49, 57, 82–83, 121, 129, 143n29,
146n6; awareness of as moral
gain of civil war, 106–7, 115;
barbarians, tribes and divisions/
lack of unity in Syria, 81–82; and
al-Bustani's innovative terminology, 10; as cause of civil war,
92–93, 94; and drum analogy,
84, 138n1; overcoming as path to
civilization, 121, 130; plural form
(*al-aghradh*), 60–61, 143n29
ghayat (self-interests), 60, 61, 81, 120
the Golden Calf story, 70, 145n3
Great Powers, 4, 64–65, 147n1
Guizot, François, 32
Gülhane Reform Edict of 1839,
19, 55

Hadiqat al-Akhbar (newspaper), 24,
47, 56, 134n6, 139n10

Hakim, Carol, 21, 39
the Hamadas (Shiʿa vassals), 13
al-Hanin ila al-awtan (Longing for
one's homelands), 54
haraka (movement, unrest), 132n18
al-harb al-ahliyya (civil war
neologism), 6, 10
Hatt-i Hümayun of 1856
(Ottoman reform decree), 28,
29, 38, 135n27
hawadith (events), 132n18
Heine, Heinrich, 7
Hill, Peter, 52
historical memory, construction
of, 3–4
*Historical Treatise on the Conditions
of Mount Lebanon in Its Feudal
Age*, 46
homeland. See *al-watan*
hoodlums (*awbash*), 58
"horticultural trio" of journals,
32–33
Hourani, Albert, 14, 36–37
hubb (love/attachment), 41, 54, 57
hubb al-watan (patriotism/
love of the homeland): *See
also al-watan*; a compatriot's
primary duty, 77; as a contract
of rights and duties, 58; as
antidote to sectarianism, 10, 39,
54; Arab nationalism and love
of Syria, 36, 39, 41, 54, 76–78;
domestic love and equality, 26,
134n13; as driver of progress,
civilization and happiness, 77,
129; as faith, 50, 56–57, 142n16,
143n17, 145n3b
human being (*al-insan*), 58
humanitarian intervention, 4, 29,
65–66, 68–69, 97
human rights, 58
hunting rights, 19

Ibn Khaldun, *51*, 145n1c, 148n2c
Ibn Manzur, Muhammad ibn
    Mukarram, *54*
Ibrahim Pasha, General (Egypt),
    15, 144n1
identity (Arab): as alterable,
    modern and hybrid, 40, 59; in
    colonial context, 40; rhetorical
    and literary construction of,
    40–41; and sectarianism, 39–40,
    60; Syrian, 22, 24, 46, 119, 139n7
identity of interests, 102, 147n3b
al-ʿilla (source/cause), 137n15
ʿillat al-dhamm (source of
    attachment), 39
al-ʿilla wa al-maʿlul (cause
    and effect), 137n15
al-iman (faith), 57, 143n18
al-insan (human being), 58
International Commission of
    Inquiry, 21, 144n1, 145n1
Israfil (the archangel of death),
    45–46, 139n4
Italian city-states, and Fakhr
    al-Din, II, 15
*Iterations of Loss: Mutilation and
    Aesthetic Form, al-Shidyaq to
    Darwish*, 43

al-Jabarti, ʿAbd al-Rahman, 3
al-Jahiz, Abu Uthman, 54
"Jamaican Letter," 7
al-Janna (Paradise), 32
Jessup, Henri, 25
Jesuits, and national boundary-
    drawing by Christian essence
    and cultural ownership, 54
al-Jinan (The Gardens): foun-
    dation of, 30; as laboratory
    of social reform and cultural
    revival, 32–33; Ottoman closure
    of, 8; patriotism as faith, 50; and

semantic shift from kinship to
    nationality, 49
al-jinsiyya: as attachment to nation-
    state, 49; al-Bustani's definition,
    140n19; and racial stereotyping,
    49–50, 96, 113
al-jins (race): diversity and not
    looking through the lens of
    race, 109; shifts in meaning
    since *Nafir Suriyya*, 49–50,
    140n20
Judgment Day (*yawm al-nafir*),
    45–46, 79, 139n4
Jumblat, Bashir, 16
Jumblat, Saʿid Bey, 21
the Jumblats (Druze leaders), 16, 21,
    82, 146n4, 148n1
Jumblat-Yazbaki factionalism, 82,
    146n4
al-Junayna (Little Garden), 32
justice: to be left to constituted
    authorities, 69, 84; civil war
    and factionalism as negation
    of, 61, 80, 112; and compensation/
    relief for damages, 69–70,
    84, 145n3; and Ottoman
    reform, 68
justification by faith doctrine, 25

Karam, Yusuf, 146n1c
Kesrouany, Maya, 42
*Kharabat Suriyya, the Ruins of
    Syria*, 47
al-khasaʾir al-adabiyya (moral-
    cultural losses), 37
Khazin muqataʿjis (Maronite), 20
al-khirba (ruinous event), 6
Khitab, 36
Khitab fi al-hayʾa al-ijtimaʿiyya
    (al-Bustani reform text), 41
al-Khuri, Khalil, 24, 47, 52, 134n6,
    139n10

Khutba fī ādāb al-ʿArab (al-Bustani
reform text), 36, 41, 46,
140nn21-23
Kisrawan district, popular
uprisings, 19–20
Koselleck, Reinhart, 54, 60
Küçük Kaynarca Peace Treaty
(1774), 16

Lammens, Henri, 48
Lebanon system of political
representation (*al-taʾifiyya*), 59
Leil, Charles, 8
Les Phüniciens et l'Odysüe, 48
Lewis, Bernard, 53
liars/lying and racial stereotyping,
99–101, 147n2b
Lisan al-ʿArab, 54
Lisan al-Hal newspaper, 24
Lord Palmerston, 5
love (attachment/*hubb*), 41,
54, 57
"Love of the homeland is an
Element of Faith," 50, 56–57, 77,
142n16, 143n17, 145n3b

Maʿani. *See* Fakhr al-Din II
al-Maʿani
al-Madrasa al-Wataniyya
(the National School), 30–32
Makdisi, Ussama, 8, 28, 38,
39–40, 62
march of history, 6
Maronite College in Rome, 24
Maronites: the al-Bustanis as,
134n3; vs. emir factionalism,
16, 65; equality discourse
against Druze landlords, 19;
and Fakhr al-Din's emirate, 15;
and French Catholic ties, 18;
impact of the National School
on clergy, 31; intra-community

peasant-landlord conflict, 18;
and killing of Shidyaq, 27–28;
labor migration, 17, 23; myth of
"privileges and traditions" and
entitlement to Mount Lebanon,
18; revenge seeking of, 145n1; as
tax collectors, 15; victimology
and French intervention, 21–22,
66, 133n26
Marx, Karl, 4–5
Matar, Elias, 47
The Meaning of Disaster (C. Zurayk,
1948), 3–4
Mehmed Ali Pasha, 55
Midhat Pasha, and closure of
al-Jinan, 8
al-milla, 53
"millet system" of law, 141n4
Mill, James S., 147n3b
mimicry, 126–27
modern colonial subjectivity:
and ambivalence, 3–4; and
community of suffering, 47; of
destruction and loss, 43–44;
double consciousness and self-
colonization, 41; and doubt,
36–37, 137n4; and guilt and moral
sensibility, 42
modern concepts before the word,
141n4
modernity and non-Western
historiography, 40
modern state, 56–57, 81
Mongol sacking of Baghdad, 3
morals (*al-akhlaq*). *See al-adab/
adabi*
muhibb al-watan (patriot), 56
Muhit al-Muhit (Arabic lexicon),
33–34, 45
Mukhtara trial, 148n1
al-Mutanabbi, 9
mythology of doctrines, 141n3

al-nafir, origin and meaning of
term, 10, 45, 46
Nafir Suriyya: *See also* rights of man;
authorship, 2, 6–7; Bakhtinian
reading of, 41; binary categories
in, 37; civil war as context for,
1–2, 144nn1-2; discontinuance
of, 29–30; emancipatory vision
of, xiv; historiography and
reception of, 35–39; rhetorical
style of, 2, 37, 41; significance of,
1–2, 5–6; still relevant in Arab
nationalism debates, 42
Nahda: in Beirut, 7–8, 33; al-Bustani
as key figure in, 23; critical
studies, 40–41; and gardens as
ideal political space and community, 32, 136n40; inspiration
from the French revolutions,
55–56; *Nafir Suriyya* as a key text
in, 1; and Syrian nation concept,
47, 140n15; and women, 26, 27
Nahdawis, "double consciousness"
of, 41
Nahdawis: as guardians of Arab
future, 43–44, 138n30; and racial
stereotypes, 50
Nakba (Palestinian), 3
Napoleon, III, 5
Napoleon Bonaparte, 3
the National School (al-Madrasa
al-Wataniyya), 30–32, 108, 148n2
Native Church of Beirut, 26, 27,
134n18
New Imperialism, 8
New York Daily Tribune, 5
Nicholas, Czar, 5
Nouvelle gùographie universelle, 48

Orientalism: and Arab anti-sectarianism, xiii; and culture talk/
clash-of-civilization narratives,
52; internalized self-colonization, 41; in *Nafir Suriyya,* 2;
Ottoman, 137n17; as Ottoman
nostalgia, 53; and psychological
stereotypes of Arabs, 4; and
stereotypes of "wild tribes," 5, 51
Ottoman-British reintegration
of Mount Lebanon into Bilad
al-Sham, 18
Ottoman Empire: and Fakhr
al-Din, II, 15; as guarantor of
the homeland, 2, 58, 68, 145n2c;
pacification of Druze leaders, 21,
144n1, 148nn1,1b,1c; and politics
of notables, 14; post-occupation
reorganization and Druze
notables, 18–19; reform decree
(Hatt-i Hümayun of 1856), 28,
29, 38, 135n27; tax concessions
and Fakhr al-Din's attempted
secession, 15
Ottoman-European free trade
agreements, 43
Ottoman Imperial Rescript of 1839.
See Gülhane Reform Edict of
1839; Tanzimat reforms
Ottoman Orientalism, 40, 137n17
Ottoman reform: *See also* Tanzimat
reforms; al-Bustani's support
for, 28–29; as challenge to
traditional governmentality,
146n3b; discourse of equality
in, 19; in *Nafir Suriyya,* 2; and
popular uprisings, 17–20

patience, 68–70, 70, 145n3
la patrie, 53, 55
patriot. *See* compatriot; *hubb
al-watan*
patriot, false, 57–58
the people (*al-sha'ab*), 58
petitions, battle of, 18–19

popular and peasant uprisings,
17–20, 40
prejudice. See *al-gharadh*
print capitalism, and nationalism,
138n25
progress: *See also* economic development; civilization, 77, 88, 106,
124, 128; and colonialist thinking,
40, 137n17; and merit-based
leadership/administration, 116;
and *al-watan,* 37
Protestantism, 25–26, 27, 40. *See also*
American mission/missionaries;
Protestant seminary of ʿAbayh, 27
Prussia, position on humanitarian
intervention, 5

Qaysi-Yamani factionalism, 22, 82,
146n4
Qissat Asʿad Shidyaq, 28
Queen Zenobia,, 140n15

Reclus, Elisée, 48
refugees, 29, 68–69, 144n1, 146n1c
religion(s): *See also* factionalism;
fanaticism; al-gharadh; sectarianism; as a means to civilization, 128; Egyptian occupation
and enmity between, 17–18; as
equal before Ottoman reform
laws, 54, 135n27; freedom and
equality of, 36; imaginable
national territory unbounded
by, 53–54; living (mutually
respectful), 95–96; and lying,
100; as morally beneficial, 90–91;
as necessarily separated from
political authority, 2, 36, 38, 96,
107, 117–18; and partisanship, 83;
and rights, 60, 74–75; Syria as a
Babel of, 36, 57, 120; true, 60, 74,
100, 128

Reşid Pasha, Mustafa, 55
revolutions: and Antilyas revolutionary discourse, 18, 142n13; and
civil war, 3, 131n7, 142n12; French
as inspiration for al-Tahtawi
and al-Bustani, 55, 142nn11,13
al-riʿaya (subjects), relationship to
the state/homeland, 58, 143n23
right of vengeance, 97, 144n1
rights: to compensation/relief for
damages, 69–70, 84, 145n3; and
duties to *al-watan* (homeland),
29, 55, 58, 77, 129; human, 58;
and humanitarian intervention,
69; hunting, 19; to life, honor
and prosperity, 77, 145n2b; and
religion, 60, 74–75
rights of man (*huquq al-insan*): as
bourgeois, 2; and European
intervention, 66, 133n26; and
freedom of conscience, 95–96;
and the French Revolution,
55–56; sectarianism as negation
of, 70, 80
rings/chain of global interdependence, 109–10, 145n1b
Robinson Crusoe, 42
ruinous event (*al-khirba*), 6
rule of law: in al-Bustani's bourgeois deference to, 2, 41, 42,
115–16; and equality, 36; and
European intervention, 66; as
guarantee of rights, 95, 96, 111
Russia, 5

Sacks, Jeffrey, 43–44
Salibi, Kamal, 13
al-Saq ʿala al-saq, 34
Sarmiento, Domingo, 7
sectarianism: and Arab identity,
39–40, 60; as a threat to the
homeland, 60, 67, 78, 80–81,

106–7; Christian, 40; the concept before the word, 59, 62, 133n18; definition, 39–40; *hubb al-watan* as antidote to, 10, 39, 54, 59; incompatibility with modern civilization, 121; institutionalization of in Lebanon, 19, 59, 133n18; as prejudice (*al-gharadh*), 49, 60–61, 143n29

sectarian system of political representation in Lebanon (*al-ta'ifyya*), 59

sectarian violence, 30, 39, 137n13, 141n4

"Seek the host—not the house," 58, 77

self: *See also* modern colonial subjectivity; cultivation of, 123–25; demonized in liberal subject, 42; emancipation, 30, 33

Self-Criticism after the Defeat (S. al-'Azm), 4

self-interests (*ghayat*), 60, 61, 81, 120

separation of religious and political authority, 2, 36, 38, 96, 107, 117–18

sex/sexuality and *al-jins* concept, 140n20

al-sha'ab (the people), 58

Shahin, Tanyus (Maronite commoner-rebel), 20

Sharabi, Hisham, 37

Sheehi, Stephen, 40–41

al-Shidyaq, Ahmad Faris, 43, 49, 57

Shidyaq, As'ad abduction and death, 27–28

Shidyaq, Tannus, 14, 20, 22

Shihabi emirate: and confessional ambivalence, 17; and Druze-Maronite cooperation, 13–14, 19; and Egyptian occupation, 17–18; popular and peasant upris-

ings against, 16; and *Sonderweg* narrative, 14

the Shuf social order, 17, 23

Silk, Cotton and the Rise of the Arabic Novel (E. Holt), 42

silk trade: and Beirut *Nahda,* 33; and capital accumulation in Beirut, 42–43; and Maronite labor migration, 17, 23

Skinner, Quentin, 141n3

Smith, Eli, Dr., 25, 28, 46–47, 49, 134n16

Smith, Sarah, 26

social contract. *See* rights

social welfare. *See* welfare of the homeland

Sonderweg (al-Yaziji) narrative, 14

state of barrenness (nature), 123

subjects (*al-ri'aya*), legal concepts of, 58–59

Sunni-Shia rivalry discourse, 3, 6

Suriyya (Syria), meaning and history of term, 46

Syria: *See also* Arab nationalism; as a Babel of religions, 36, 57, 120; ancient, 46, 119, 139n7; antiquity narrative (as Christian), 47–49; al-Bustani and Khuri on, 47; as al-Bustani's *watan,* 36; as community of suffering, 47; entering the modern era, 119–21; as identity and affective community, 22, 24; modern crisis, 39; political semantics of, 46–47, 139n6; western vs. *Nahda* concepts of, 48

"Syrian nation," 39, 47–48

Syrian Protestant College, 8, 31, 47

Syrian Scientific Society, 31–32

ta'assub (fanaticism), 36

tahazzubat (factionalism). *See* factionalism

al-Tahtawi, Rif'at al-Rifa'i
(Egyptian reformer): and
Arab nationalism, 36, 53; and
French Enlightenment, 56;
and the French revolutions,
55–56, 142nn11,13; and
al-gharadh, 144n29; influence
on al-Bustani, 56–57
ta'ifa/tawa'if (animal collectives),
59–60. *See also* bees
al-ta'ifiyya (sectarian system of
political representation in
Lebanon), 59
ta'ifiyya/tawa'if (animal
collectives), 59–60
Taj al-'Arus, 54
al-ta'lim (education), 50
al-tamaddun (civilization).
See civilization
Tanzimat reforms: Gülhane
Reform Edict of 1839, 55, 145n2b;
Hatt-i Hümayun, 28, 29, 38,
135n27; and the "millet system"
of law, 141n4; and sectarian
violence, 137n13; state-subject
relationship in, 58
technology and the chain/rings of
interdependence, 109–10, 145n1b
"The Address to the German
Nation," 7
Thomson, William, 30
Tibawi, Abdulatif, 37
transconfessional contract, 54
true homeland, 79, 138n2
true religion, 60, 74, 100, 128
trumpet (*al-buq*), 45, 139nn3-4.
See also clarion

al-umma, 53
'uqala' (responsible thinkers), 58
urban utopia, al-Bustani's
civilization as, 51, 124–26

Vaterland, 53
virtue: and anti-sectarianism, 109;
autoemancipatory and self-
reflective, 30, 33; as civilization
and cultivation of self, 123–25;
and true (ecumenical) religion,
74, 95

Wadi al-Taym, murder of
Shihabis, 20
al-watan (homeland): See also
hubb al-watan; a "chain of many
rings," 76; as alternative to
sectarianism, 39, 54, 59; and
al-Bustani's innovative language,
10; as challenge to imperialist
religious territorial divisions,
54; cognates of, 53, 141n4;
deserving ('uqala') and unde-
serving *awbash* the homeland,
58, 77–78; and Judgment Day, 79,
138n2; loss of, 92, 147n2; morals
of people determine value of,
76–77; and necessity of concord,
94; and politics of rights and
duties, 29, 55, 77; as protean
Arab nationalism, 37; semantic
evolution of, 54
wataniyyat, Nafir Suriyya pamphlets
as, 45, 46, 56
al-wataniyya vs. *al-qawmiyya*, 48,
140n17
welfare of the homeland: and
Arabic as language of instruction, 120; and collective impact
of civil war/factionalism, 67;
dependent on modern system
of governance, 81; as dependent
on patriotism and freedoms/
rights, 58, 77, 129; importance
of patriotic leaders, 128;
prejudice as a threat to, 60,

67, 78, 80–81, 106–7; reformed
Ottoman state as guarantor of,
2, 58, 68, 145n2c
Western civilization, 2–5, 125, 127
Western imperialism: and defining
territorial/national boundaries,
53–54; and exploitation of
diversity, xiv; and the representation of indigenous national
past, 40
"wild tribes" stereotype, 5
women, 26, 27, 108, 125

work-ethic, and civilization, 42,
51, 104

Yanni, Jurji, 47
al-Yaziji, Nasif, 14, 20, 22, 46, 134n6,
138n30
Young Turk Revolution, 48

al-Zabidi, Murtada, 54
Zokak al-Blat (Beirut
neighborhood), 24
Zurayk, Constantin, 3–4

www.ingramcontent.com/pod-product-compliance
Ingram Content Group UK Ltd.
Pitfield, Milton Keynes, MK11 3LW, UK
UKHW042045170425
457604UK00002B/84